BREXIT and its Consequences for UK and EU Citizenship
or Monstrous Citizenship

Nijhoff Law Specials

VOLUME 94

The titles published in this series are listed at *brill.com/nlsp*

BREXIT and its Consequences for UK and EU Citizenship or Monstrous Citizenship

By

Elspeth Guild

Jean Monnet Professor ad personam
Queen Mary University of London, Law

BRILL

NIJHOFF

LEIDEN | BOSTON

The Library of Congress Cataloging-in-Publication Data is available online at http://catalog.loc.gov

Typeface for the Latin, Greek, and Cyrillic scripts: "Brill". See and download: brill.com/brill-typeface.

ISBN 978-90-04-34088-6 (paperback)
ISBN 978-90-04-34089-3 (e-book)

Printed by Printforce, the Netherlands

Contents

Acknowledgements

There are many people who have played an important role in the writing of this book. First and foremost I must thank my partner, Didier Bigo, Sciences-Po and Kings College London for all the wonderful discussions and debates about the subject and for his valuable insights from a continental perspective into many of the political issues. Our discussions about the image of the monster were central to the form this book has taken. Second, I must thank emeritus Professor Kees Groenendijk, Radboud University Nijmegen (NL) with whom many long discussions and debates have provided me with invaluable insights into the relations of the UK with the other Member States particularly in the field of free movement of persons.

My Head of Department, Professor Valsamis Mitsilegas, has provided me with invaluable support and encouragement throughout the process and pushed me to write this book to present at my inaugural lecture, (five years after my recruitment) at Queen Mary University of London. He agreed to act as a discussant at the lecture providing me with important new insights which I have woven into the text. Similarly Professor Sionaidh Douglas-Scott agreed to be a discussant and from her deep knowledge of British constitutionalism, raised important issues about the nature of sovereignty in the UK which have deepened my thinking. Emeritus Professor Carol Harlow, LSE, kindly agreed to chair my inaugural lecture but went far beyond the exigencies of that role and both read and provided me with important comments and suggestions on the text. I must also thank Professor Marina Warner, All Souls College University of Oxford and Birkbeck College University of London, for the inspiration of her Reith Lectures 1994. Her deployment of the image of the monster has inspired my investigation into BREXIT.

Finally, I must thank all my colleagues and students in London, Nijmegen, Paris and Bruges for their fascinating reflections, comments and questions which have enriched my thinking and my editor, Lindy Melman, with whom it is always a delight to work.

Elspeth Guild
September 2016

List of Abbreviations

BREXIT:	The referendum held in the UK on 23 June 2016 on whether to remain or leave the European Union – including the negotiations, campaign and after events around the voters' decision
Citizens Directive:	Directive 2004/38/EC of the European Parliament and of the Council of 29 April 2004 on the right of citizens of the Union and their family members to move and reside freely within the territory of the Member States amending Regulation (EEC) No 1612/68 and repealing Directives 64/221/EEC, 68/360/EEC, 72/194/EEC, 73/148/EEC, 75/34/EEC, 75/35/EEC, 90/364/EEC, 90/365/EEC and 93/96/EEC
CJEU:	Court of Justice of the European Union (used also for the ECJ – European Court of Justice as it was before 1 December 2009)
ECHR;	European Convention of Human Rights
ECtHR:	European Court of Human Rights
EEA:	European Economic Area
EHRC:	Equality and Human Rights Commission (UK)
EU:	European Union (including its predecessors: European Economic Community and European Community)
EU 8:	Czech Republic, Estonia, Hungary, Lithuania, Latvia, Poland, Slovakia and Slovenia
EUCFR:	European Union Charter of Fundamental Rights
EU citizen:	Citizen of the European Union
IMF:	International Monetary Fund
ISIS:	Islamic State in Iraq and Syria
MEP:	Member of the European Parliament
TEU:	Treaty on European Union
TFEU:	Treaty on the Functioning of the European Union
NATO:	North Atlantic Treaty Organisation
UK:	United Kingdom

List of Cases

European Court of Human Rights

East African Asians v UK [1973] 3 EHRR 76

Court of Justice of the European Union (chronological order by case number)

Case 43/75 *Defrenne* [1976] ECR 455
267/83 *Diatta* [1984] ECR 567
C-68/86 *UK v Council* [1988] ECR 855
C-370/90 *Surinder Singh* [1992] ECR I-4265
C-85/96 *Martinez Sala* [1998] ECR I-2691
C-192/99 *Kaur* [2001] ECR I-1237
C-291/05 *Eind* [2007] ECR I-10719.
C-127/08 *Metock* [2008] ECR I-6241
C-135/08 *Rottmann* [2010] ECR I-1449
C-459/99 *MRAX* [2002] ECR I-5691
C-109/01 *Akrich* [2003] ECR I-9607
C-157/03 *Commission v Spain* [2005] ECR I-2911
C-34/09 *Zambrano* [2011] ECR I-1177
C-456/12 *O* 12 March 2014
C-457/12 *S* 12 March 2014
C-244/13 *Ogieriakhi* 10 July 2014
C-28/12 *Commission v Council* 29 June 2015

UK National Courts

R (on the application of Baiai and others) v Secretary of State for the Home Department [2008] UKHL 53
Pham v Secretary of State for the Home Department [2015] UKSC 19.

Introduction

> Monsters breed in this terrible playground
> of fabricated identity, and all the hostile
> strategems of labelling and differentiation...
> for the vindication of us against them...
> England against Brussels and Strasbourg.
>
> MARINA WARNER, *Managing Monsters: Six Myths of Our Time –*
> *The Reith Lectures 1994*

This book examines the consequences of the UK vote on 23 June 2016 to leave the European Union on EU citizenship. The simple fact which appears to result from this vote is that within a fairly short period of time – not less than two years from the commencement of the departure procedure provided for in Article 50 TEU – British citizens will cease to be citizens of the European Union while the nationals of the other 27 will continue to have this status. Thus nationals of the other 27 Member States will continue to have the rights which attach to EU citizenship but British citizens will cease to have these rights. British citizens will retain only their British citizenship which is based on the principle of allegiance to the sovereign – the foundation of state sovereignty – not on the principle of rights as is the case with EU citizenship. So what was so terrible about these EU citizenship rights? This question is at the heart of my book.

The construction and image of the monster and the monstrous form are my metaphorical frameworks to understand what happened to the EU project in the UK that led to the vote in June and what this means for all of us as citizens. St George is the patron saint of England, that part of the UK whose people were decisive in determining the outcome of the 23 June 2016 referendum.[1] St George is normally portrayed slaying a dragon – he is the monster killer. Usually, he is mounted on a horse and his lance is piercing the monstrous dragon which has been the cause of so much suffering to the people, the English. The image of the threatening monster is central to English religious identity and the victory of St George over his monster is a fixture of the socio-political landscape of England.

---

[1]   In England 53.4% of the votes were to leave the EU (15,188,406); in Northern Ireland 44.2% of the votes were to leave (349,442); in Scotland 38.0% of the votes were to leave (854,572) http://www.bbc.com/news/politics/eu_referendum/results visited 5 September 2016.

The 1870 mosaic in the Central Lobby of the Palace of Westminster which greets British members of Parliament each day when they enter depicts St George as designed by Sir Edward Poynter. St George stands in full armour, the slain dragon at his feet. The figure of Fortitude stands on his right carrying a club and a lion's skin. Purity is on his left bearing white lilies and the saint's helmet. In the iconography of the BREXIT campaign, the EU was presented as a truly monstrous entity, sucking out British state sovereignty from the British polity[2] and enslaving the British people with foreign laws.[3] The vote to leave was presented as a vote for liberty and the independence of Britain as opposed to remaining in the thrall of the monstrous EU.[4] Yet when one steps away from the sacred image of St George and his monster and one examines the more secular monsters of our common mythology and the stories we tell our children, the picture is quite different. Europa and Zeus in the form of her monster bull are positive images which produce Europe. Beauty discovers the excellent qualities of her beast and once kissed, the toad turns into a prince. Monsters can also be no more than our own misunderstanding of the qualities of others. Returning briefly, to sacred imagery, the hero of St George and the dragon depends on the belief structure of the viewer. The tremendous popularity of the image of St George in Haiti as documented by Metraux[5] resulted from the presence of the dragon, Damballa, the serpent spirit in Haitian traditional belief. In one form of the story, Damballa, through his sacrifice, becomes divine and thereby the Great Master who creates the cosmos. For the Haitians, the dragon was the venerated subject of the image not St George.

The monstrous and the monster are frameworks of analysis which have been used by many social scientists to examine the citizen/immigrant divide. Marina Warner's *Managing Monsters* Reith Lectures in 1994 have provided me with much inspiration for this discussion. I will not try to compete with such an eminent historian nor do I enjoy the erudition in mythology to do so. Yet I am indebted to her for insights into the mon-

---

2   http://www.spectator.co.uk/2016/08/brexit-means-that-britain-will-be-boss-again/ visited 6 September 2016.

3   http://www.mirror.co.uk/news/uk-news/how-many-britains-laws-really-7420612 visited 6 September 2016.

4   Boris Johnson, leader of the Leave campaign declared that 23 June would be Independence Day for Britain https://www.youtube.com/watch?v=emxumavBU3M visited 6 September 2016.

5   Métraux, Alfred. *Voodoo in Haiti*. Vol. 341. Schocken, 1972.

ster. Rene Girard in his seminal work *Things Hidden since the Foundation of the World* (1978 in the French original) posits the monstrous double at the core of the victimage mechanism which he places at the heart of religion. While the English translation does not place the emphasis of the French original on 'le double monstrous' this is a key element of his work. For my purposes I would like to borrow from him the monstrous as a dialectic between the object and its own projected image which is perceived as terrifying, horrific and sufficiently dangerous to justify its killing. I will not take Girard's line further into the transformation of the killing into a myth of sacrifice as this exceeds my objectives. Instead I will remain in the shallow waters of the theorist with the monstrous double which is the image of the watcher but seen as deformed. This is the opposite of the Nascissus myth where the young man on seeing his image in a pond falls in love with the beautiful person in the lake mistaking the reflection for someone other than himself. Here our protagonist looks in the mirror and is terrified by his or her own image which is reflected back at him or her as monstrous. For my purposes, the monstrous image at work in the BREXIT events is that of the UK as an integral part of the EU whole – the image in the mirror is one of a complete figure not a composite of pieces separable and accessible to reconfiguration. The fixation of the UK government on abolishing the objective of the EU as an 'ever closer Union' is perhaps the most curious manifestation of this monstrous double.

I will also use the monstrous in a slightly different or extended form to help understand how the fear of the monstrous image leads in fact to the deformation of the original. The actions which are taken as a result of the perception of the monstrous end in an actual deformation of rules, procedures, rights and entitlements to the detriment of everyone. The horror which eventually convinced almost 52% of the UK voting public to reject the 'monstrous' EU pushed the British Government to insist on a series of negotiations with the other 27 Member States which deformed the constitutional rules of the EU and ended with an agreement which compromised the Commission, the European Parliament and challenged the Court of Justice to accept a tacit reversal of its constant jurisprudence. But most fundamental, for British citizenship, it deformed the process of renewal of the concept of citizenship in the UK into one of rights through the acquisition of EU citizenship.

I will examine the monstrous and BREXIT in four sections as follows:

1. The monstrous negotiations: on 19 February 2016 agreement was reached between the 27 Member States and the UK in the form of an international agreement rather than a decision of the Council,

the normal form for such agreements. The agreement set out what the EU would do to change itself and the rights of its citizens if the UK Government would campaign in the referendum (which it had championed and legislation for which it had led through the UK parliament) in favour of the UK remaining in the EU. I will look at how this extraordinary set of negotiations became a monstrous or deformed image of what negotiations among EU Member States and institutions are designed to be.

2.   Monstrous citizenships: what is the UK's problem with EU citizenship? What does citizenship mean in the UK and the EU and why is the image of one the monstrous reflection of the other? In this section I will examine British citizenship as a citizenship of obedience with limited and fluid rights easily extinguished and increasingly difficult to acquire in comparison with EU citizenship as a citizenship based exclusively on designated rights set out in binding legal texts on which its holders are entitled to rely. I will examine to what extent was it these rights which became the monstrous element of EU citizenship which was no longer tolerable and had to be extinguished.

3.   Citizens and their monstrous families: in this section I will take my analysis a little further – the monstrous as also an element of contamination of the pure. In the 19 February 2016 conclusions between the British Prime Minister and the Council, one of the key successes of the UK Government was agreement that if the referendum went in favour of the UK remaining in the EU, the EU institutions would change (by highly dubious means) the rights of EU citizens to be joined by their third country family members in accordance with the straight forward and fairly simple EU rules. The citizens who were the objects of this effort by the British Government were not primarily nationals of the 27 Member States but rather British citizens who moved to another Member State to live and/or work and enjoyed family reunion with their third country national family members there. So long as they stayed in another Member State, the UK Government could tolerate this contamination but EU law provides that after living and/or working in another Member State for a while, the family is entitled to return home to the UK bringing with them their third country national family members again under the simple, straight forward (and cheap) EU rules. These British citizens become the monstrous ones with monstrous family members who get access to the UK through monstrous means.

4.   Monstrous fears: the referendum campaign in the UK was led both
     for the remain and leave campaigns by politicians who promised
     catastrophe, disaster and disorder to those who voted in the op-
     posite way proposed by the relevant politician. Economic disaster
     was a favorite of the remain campaign, social disaster in the form
     of uncontrolled immigration – the dog whistle for racism and xen-
     ophobia – was the big seller for the leave campaign. Fears puffed
     up by rhetoric became the norm. Just as young people in particu-
     lar enjoy being frightened by horror movies while at the same time
     claiming that the movie was silly and ridiculously unbelievable, so
     the British public began to amuse itself with monstrous fears and
     the politicians leading the two campaigns became ever more ex-
     travagant in their fearful claims as if daring the public to disbelieve
     them as if they were teenagers at the horror movies. Both political
     camps shared the anti-immigration argument though in differing
     intensities. This section will examine how the fear of the EU citizen
     became the fear of uncontrolled immigration and the effects on the
     negotiations. The antidote to monstrous fears is truth and trans-
     parency, little of which were on show during the campaign. Expert
     opinion, one of the modern forms of establishing truth claims, was
     ridiculed and denigrated by the Leave campaign. Informed policy
     making was discarded and expertise itself became portrayed as
     monstrous, constituting an obstacle to the maintenance of preju-
     dice and intolerance. Expertise and experts became the dragon to
     be slain by a valiant St George figure, driven by blind faith in the
     innate superiority of the British people.

I will conclude this examination of the monstrous BREXIT debate with
some reflections on where the UK may go from here. Two things have
been particularly clear in the aftermath of the referendum, first, the political class in the centre – both right and left – suffered grave and immediate implosions. While the ruling Conservative Party pulled itself together
(at least at the time of writing) and managed to replace the Prime Minister more quickly and with less trauma than originally feared, the effect on
the political class is on-going and enormous. This impact has already had
important knock on effects with an astonishing about face by the (new)
Prime Minster to reconsider the biggest infrastructure project in Europe
– the new nuclear project at Hinckley Point in the UK which is planned
to be carried out by the French energy company EDF and financed by a
Chinese company close to the Chinese authorities. The decision to recon-

sider the investment (which many had considered financially ruinous for the UK) was taken after the Chinese representatives had already arrived in the UK for signature of the documentation. They had to pack up and leave again with nothing. The French company, EDF, almost came to grief over the proposed project with a series of high level officials resigning over it on the basis that it would bring down the company. The French minister obliged all the members of EDF's board representing the state's stake in the company to vote for the project. EDF also had to go home with nothing. This curiously high handed treatment of foreign investors is quite surprising from a British Government which has been highly motivated to encourage foreign investment. (In September 2016, after the British Prime Minister met her Chinese counterpart at the G20 meeting in Beijing, she changed her mind about the project and the deal once again this time approving a version of it).[6] Secondly, the integrity of the UK which seemed to have been resolved after the Scottish independence referendum in 2014 is suddenly again in question.[7]

The capacity of the EU referendum result to bind the whole of the UK remains to be seen. Scotland and the Scottish Nationalist Party will be a key player in the next developments. But already speculation which would have been unimaginable even two months before the referendum is suddenly normal, for instance, should Northern Ireland hold a referendum to join the Republic of Ireland? It is no longer obvious that the UK as a single entity will survive the EU referendum. The political party in power, the Conservatives, normally reluctant to contemplate devolution, is already signalling to the regions that more devolution is on the cards. Finally, one cannot overlook the immediate consequence of the referendum in the UK for ethnic minorities (both British and non-British) EU citizens and immigrants living in the UK. Towards the end of the campaign, Jo Cox, a member of Parliament who was campaigning for the Remain camp was killed in what appears to have been a politically

---

6   Hinckley Point : 15 September 2016 Press Release Government confirms Hinkley Point C project following new agreement in principle with EDF https://www.gov.uk/government/news/government-confirms-hinkley-point-c-project-following-new-agreement-in-principle-with-edf visited 28 September 2016.

7   The Scottish Parliament on BREXIT http://www.parliament.scot/General%20Documents/2016.09.26_Leaving_the_EU_-_weekly_update_26_September.pdf visited 29 September 2016.

motivated attack.[8] After the results of the referendum were announced, the reports of people walking up to strangers on the street, particularly women wearing head scarves and saying "I voted leave – now get out of my country" are truly shocking in a country which has prided itself on racial tolerance. The dog whistle effect of the Leave campaign's attacks on EU immigration was immediate. It was understood in some parts of the public as a declaration of open season for racism, intolerance and xenophobia to be openly expressed and acted upon.

---

8   https://www.theguardian.com/uk-news/2016/jun/18/thomas-mair-charged-with-
     of-mp-jo-cox visited 5 September 2016.

Monstrous Negotiations

> It seems to me that ethnic nationalism threatens civil
> harmony and the traditional tolerance of our evolving
> democracy more profoundly than any other contemporary
> story, and so I concentrate on the elements in the British
> historical imagination which resort to insularity to
> assert identity and power.
>
> MARINA WARNER, *Managing Monsters: Six Myths of Our Time –*
> *The Reith Lectures 1994*

Introduction

The UK joined the predecessor of the EU on 1 January 1973 following negotiations undertaken by a Conservative Government. The UK had originally applied to join the predecessor of the EU in August 1961 but that
application was unsuccessful. After its successful arrival into the EU, the
UK had doubts. It held a referendum on whether to stay in the Union on
7 June 1975 and voted largely to remain a Member State. Like many Member States, the UK has had its ups and downs with the EU, not least as a
strong supporter of deregulation of markets but less enthusiastic about
common policies around immigration and criminal justice. Both the tra-
ditionally important UK political parties, Labour and the Conservatives,
have had their EU supporters and detractors within their ranks – the size
of those opposed to the EU has risen and fallen over the history of the
UK's membership. When the Labour party came to power in 1997 after
the long reign of Mrs Thatcher, the (then) new Prime Minister, Tony Blair,
embarked on a strongly pro EU route.[1] The invasion of Iraq in 2003 championed by the UK Government in support of their US allies but strongly
opposed by the French Government became something of a turning
point in the UK's enthusiasm for the EU.[2] The UK invested substantial
resources in the creation of a 'coalition of the willing' to participate in the
invasion after the French Government made a UN Security Council Reso-

---

[1]   MacShane Denis *BREXIT, How Britain Left Europe* IB Taurus, London 2016 pp.
84-104.

[2]   Lowe, Vaughan. "The Iraq Crisis: What Now?" *International and Comparative Law
Quarterly* 52.04 (2003): 859-871.

lution approving the invasion impossible. A number of Central and Eastern European countries which were about to become EU Member States on 1 May 2004 were persuaded to join the effort. In the same time period, the UK's (then) Minister of Foreign Affairs, Jack Straw, announced that the UK would not apply transitional measures to delay the free movement of workers from the Central and Eastern European states (the so called EU 8)[3] joining the EU to come to the UK and work there. Under the accession agreements, the transitional measures could be applied for a maximum of seven years. Ireland and Sweden, among the pre-2004 Member States also did not apply transitional measures. Subsequently the UK Government would argue that a worker registration scheme put into place to track where workers from the EU 8 were working in the UK was a mandatory transitional measure and extended for the full seven years permitted under the accession agreements. The UK's engagement with the EU through the early 2000s and the tension created by the UK's support of the US led invasion of Iraq in the face of French (and German) opposition was central. The political imaginary image of the UK as somewhere in the mid Atlantic between the USA and continental Europe took hold. On account of political investment in what was to be a highly controversial military engagement in Iraq (and the wider region) supporting the US administration of the time, the UK political consciousness appears to have moved west.

Where did the Referendum Idea Come from?

On 22 January 2013 in the face of a general election, the leader of the Conservatives, David Cameron, promised the UK public that if re-elected he would call a referendum on the continued membership of the UK in the EU. His party had been in a coalition government with the pro-EU Liberal-Democrats since May 2010. Prime Minister Cameron's argument was that the EU needed fundamental reform and powers needed to be returned to the UK to determine its sovereign fate.[4] The meaning of sovereignty as used by the Prime Minister and as revealed in the negotiations

---

3   Czech Republic, Estonia, Hungary, Latvia, Lithuania, Poland, Slovakia and Slovenia.

4   Douglas-Scott, Sionaidh. "A UK Exit from the EU: The End of the United Kingdom or a New Constitutional Dawn?" *Cambridge Journal of International and Comparative Law* (2015).

is not democratic sovereignty or popular sovereignty.[5] As became apparent in the mechanism which he would require for the agreement which excluded all democratic scrutiny at national or EU levels, for him in these negotiations, sovereignty meant the right of the Prime Minister, exercising the powers of the sovereign, to act. He stated that disillusionment with the EU was at an all time high in the UK and that the people were entitled to have their say on whether the UK should leave. He undertook that, if elected, he would pursue negotiations with the EU to get a new deal for the UK for the repatriation of powers and if he got a good deal from the others he would campaign whole heartedly for the UK to stay in the EU.[6] In the elections held on 8 May 2015, the Conservatives obtained an absolute majority in parliament.

On 27 May 2015, the Queen's Speech – the mechanism for the British government to announce forthcoming legislative plans - included a bill for a referendum on the UK's membership of the EU. At the European Council meeting on 25-26 May, the (then) new Prime Minister held discussions informally with his counterparts explaining that he would be seeking a new arrangement with the EU and would be calling a referendum for this purpose. The Council Conclusions of that meeting merely state: "The UK Prime Minister set out his plans for an (in/out) referendum in the UK. The European Council agreed to revert to the matter in December."[7] The European Commission established a new unit with specific responsibility for the UK and its referendum. The Referendum Bill received first reading in the House of Commons on 28 May 2015 and Royal Assent on 17 December 2015. The territorial scope of the referendum was limited to the UK and Gibraltar (excluding other UK territories).

Who Could Vote?

Those entitled to vote, according to the Act, were British, Irish and Commonwealth citizens over the age of 18 who were resident in the United Kingdom, and British nationals resident overseas for less than 15 years, provided they appeared on the register of Parliamentary electors. Thus

---

5   Walker, Rob BJ. *Out of Line: Essays on the Politics of Boundaries and the Limits of Modern Politics*. Routledge, 2015.

6   Full text of the speech available at: http://www.bbc.com/news/uk-politics-21148282.

7   http://www.consilium.europa.eu/en/press/press-releases/2015/06/26-euco-conclusions/ visited 12 August 2016.

non-British EU citizens resident in the UK were excluded from the vote
except for Cypriot and Maltese nationals who are also Commonwealth
citizens and Irish nationals who are entitled to vote in parliamentary
elections in the UK. So nationals of three (non British) EU Member States
were entitled to vote and nationals of the remaining 24 were excluded irrespective of the length of their residence in the UK. Also excluded were
British citizens who have lived overseas for more than 15 years. Two British citizens resident in other Member States who fell outside the 15 year
rule challenged their exclusion from the right to vote in the referendum.
The case was fast tracked through the UK judicial system moving from
the High Court to the Court of Appeal then to the Supreme Court in a
couple of months and dismissed at every level. The appellants claimed
that their disenfranchisement constituted a unjustified restriction of
their EU law rights to move and reside within the territory of the Member States and separately that the common law affords protection to their
right to vote as British citizens and full members of the United Kingdom.
In refusing to hear the case, the Supreme Court stated:

> We should make it clear that the question is not whether this par-
> ticular voting exclusion is justifiable as a proportionate means of
> achieving a legitimate aim. The question is instead, firstly, wheth-
> er European Union law applies at all, as only if it does so is there
> any possibility of attacking an Act of Parliament; and secondly, if
> so, whether there is any interference with the right of free move-
> ment. Assuming for the sake of argument that European Union law
> does apply, we have decided that it is not arguable that there is an
> interference with right of free movement, for the reasons given by
> the Divisional Court and the Court of Appeal. We do have consider-
> able sympathy for the situation in which the applicants find them-
> selves and we understand that this is something which concerns
> them deeply. But we cannot discern a legal basis for challenging this
> statute. Accordingly the application for permission to appeal is re-
> fused.[8]

Thus the Supreme Court found in favour of state sovereignty – EU law
was not necessarily applicable so the court was not required to make a
reference to the CJEU. Yet, the Supreme Court was unsettled. It deter-

---

8   https://www.supremecourt.uk/news/permission-to-appeal-decision-24-may-
       2016.html visited 12 August 2016.

mined that even if EU law applied, the applicants would still lose. This is an astonishing statement in an inadmissibility determination limited to a few paragraphs. Its inclusion reveals a deep insecurity in the court itself about the legitimacy of its action. The question which the reader cannot avoid is why, at all, the Supreme Court referred to EU law when even such a reference could only undermine its own claim to exercise state sovereignty untrammelled by EU law.

The exclusion of 16 and 17 year olds was also questioned. In the Scottish independence referendum held on 18 September 2014, these young people were permitted to vote on the basis that it was their future which was at stake. The House of Lords sought to widen the EU referendum base to these 16 and 17 years olds but this was blocked by the House of Commons.[9] This meant that at least some Scottish young people who had voted in the Scottish independence referendum to remain in the UK moved by assurances that this would be the only way to remain in the EU were excluded from voting less than two years later on whether actually to remain in the EU.

What Did the UK Want from the EU?

In a letter dated 10 November 2015[10] addressed to the President of the EU Council, Donald Tusk, the UK Prime Minister set out the UK's demands for reform of the EU. He commenced the letter by stating that he had been undertaking negotiations with heads of state of other Member States and that he "had been encouraged in many conversations… that there is wide understanding of the concerns" which he raised. This statement was based on a whistle stop tour which the Prime Minister made of a number of EU capitals to discuss the UK demands with their leaders. Already this approach – to deal with the Member States bilaterally rather than address the Council, the traditional venue for the EU Heads of State to discuss and negotiate EU business – set the stage. The UK did not consider itself bound by the rules of the EU diplomacy game.Instead it acted on the basis that it was entitled to treat the Member States as separate

---

9   http://www.independent.co.uk/news/uk/politics/house-of-commons-votes-against-lowering-voting-age-for-eu-referendum-a6764966.html visited 12 August 2016.

10   https://www.gov.uk/government/uploads/system/uploads/attachment_data/file/475679/Donald_Tusk_letter.pdf visited 12 August 2016.

states with different views and opinions on which the UK could capital-ise when required to meet everyone in the Council. The Prime Minister reinforced his position regarding the legitimacy of this approach stating "The European Union has a long history of respecting the differences of its Member States...".

The Prime Minister set out four main areas in which he wanted reform of the EU:

1. Economic governance: the common currency of the EU is the Euro and all Member States are committed to joining the currency when the conditions permit. However, the UK has a permanent opt out from the Euro. The Prime Minister did not seek a new opt out from the Euro but rather a safeguard mechanism for those Member States not (or not yet) in the Euro. This would include a shopping list of seven requirements, perhaps most importantly that taxpay-ers in non-Euro countries should never be financially liable for op-erations to support the Eurozone as a currency.

2. Competitiveness: The Prime Minister wanted the EU to do more to fulfil three of the four fundamental freedoms of the EU – free move-ment of goods, services and capital (but see below on his demands for restrictions on the fourth freedom – of persons), the completion of the Single Market and boosting competitiveness and productiv-ity.

3. Sovereignty: the Prime Minister requested that the UK should no longer be obliged to work towards an 'ever closer union' as set out in the TEU and this exception should be framed in a formal, legally binding and irreversible way. Further he asked for an enhanced role for national parliaments enabling them to stop 'unwanted' legisla-tion. At this point the Prime Minister made express reference to a Dutch proposal "Europe where necessary, national where possible" thereby indicating where his support was coming from at least as regards one Member State. Finally, the Prime Minister sought con-firmation that national security was and would remain a sole re-sponsibility of the Member States.[11]

4. Immigration: this heading covers exclusively free movement of EU citizens. By entitling the section 'immigration' the Prime Minister expressly transformed EU citizens from citizens entitled to move in the territory of the entity to which their citizenship applies to

---

11   Bigo, Didier. "Rethinking Security at the crossroad of International Relations and Criminology." *British Journal of Criminology* (2016): azw062.

immigrants who should be required to fulfil conditions, be subject
to authorisation or not from state bureaucracies on whether they
can enter, reside, work and enjoy family reunion in the 'host' state.
The change of the language from entitlement and rights of citizens
to precarity and exclusion of foreigners is at work here. The Prime
Minister stated in the letter that he wanted "to find new arrangements to allow a Member State like the UK to restore a sense of fair-
ness to our immigration system and to reduce the current very high
level of population flows from within the EU into the UK." I will
return to the 'immigration' or citizenship issue in sections 3 and 4.

The Prime Minister finished his letter to the Council President with a section entitled Next Steps – advising the President on how the negotiations
should proceed and why. The letter, according to the Prime Minister, is
the basis for negotiations but that any deal would have to be legally binding and irreversible and "where necessary have force in the Treaties". This
would require changes to the Treaties which would have to be ratified by
all Member States in accordance with their constitutional arrangements.
The Prime Minister advised the President that the next substantive discussion would be at the December 2015 European Council meeting. The
reform, according to the British Prime Minister, would be both reasonable and in the wider interests of the EU. He reminded the President
that the UK is the EU's second largest economy and fifth biggest in the
world, ensuring that the special position which the UK was claiming was
justified on the basis of its size and importance in the world. He stated
"we bring an enormous contribution – political, economic, financial –
to the European Union." Finally, the importance of the deal is spelt out
clearly in the penultimate paragraph where the Prime Minister advised
the President that only if an agreement which was acceptable to the UK
was reached would the Prime Minister be "ready to campaign with all
my heart and soul to keep Britain inside a reformed European Union…"
The threat is clear: unless the Prime Minister would get what he and his
government considered necessary he would campaign against the UK remaining in the EU. In light of the referendum result, where the Prime
Minister got his deal and campaigned in favour of remain without con-
vincing his voters, the claim is rather bold.

How Monstrous were the Negotiations?

The December 2015 Council Meeting was dominated by the issue of free movement of persons but in a rather different context than the UK Prime Minister had framed it. The arrival of somewhat more asylum seekers in the EU in 2015 had surprised the interior ministries of some Member States and the costs of reception and dealing with the applications was rather unevenly spread across the Union. Some Member States had sought to limit access to their territory and asylum systems by re-introducing intra-Schengen border controls thus leaving asylum seekers in other Member States. This challenge for the Schengen border control free area was one of the two focuses of the December Council meeting. The other focus was terrorism following a series of attacks primarily in France in 2015 which were very worrying as tied to the rise (and perhaps fall) of ISIS in Syria and Iraq in particular.

The Conclusions of the Council meeting contain only one reference to the UK's referendum issues "The European Council had a political exchange of views on the UK plans for an (in/out) referendum. Following today's substantive and constructive debate, the members of the European Council agreed to work closely together to find mutually satisfactory solutions in all the four areas at the European Council meeting on 18-19 February 2016."[12]

On 2 February Council President Tusk sent a letter to all Members of the European Council advising them of the state of negotiations with the UK and the Council's proposal in response to the British Prime Minister's demands.[13] The President reassured his colleagues that "the line I did not cross, however, were the principles on which the European project is founded." He confirmed the view that the community of interests among the 27 and the UK were great but that there were still substantial issues ahead in the negotiations.[14] I will examine the contents of the negotiations regarding citizens of the Union and their transformation into migrants and immigrants in a later section. For the purposes of examining the monstrous nature of the negotiations I will consider here rather the

---

12   http://www.consilium.europa.eu/en/press/press-releases/2015/12/18-euco-conclusions/ visited 12 August 2016.

13   http://www.consilium.europa.eu/en/press/press-releases/2016/02/02-letter-tusk-proposal-new-settlement-uk/ visited 12 August 2016.

14   For the proposed draft decision of the Council attached to the letter see Council Document 4/16.

form of the negotiations and how they were transformed from a debate within the EU to a debate which was already taking place outside the forum of the EU and instead in the framework of international law.

The Tusk package of instruments to address the UK Prime Minister's concerns about the need for a new deal for the UK within the EU attached to his letter of 2 February 2016 became the subject of an exchange about the nature of any future deal. Various actors in the UK political scene, apparently, no longer trusted the EU institutions, Member States and legal structures to deliver a binding deal on which the UK could rely.[15] One key actor in the debate, the former British Justice Minister Michael Gove, attacked the negotiations leading to a deal as failing to fulfil the promise of 'binding' on the EU and the UK.[16] The argument he put forward was that any deal, if adopted in the framework of EU law would only be as binding as the political will of the EU. In his view this would mean that the structure of the EU as a body governed by rule of law with the CJEU as the ultimate arbiter of legality meant that the CJEU could overturn any deal as incompatible with EU law. His argument was that no deal was 'safe' until it escape the legal order of the EU and became impervious to a negative judgment of the CJEU. Further, the UK's need for 'speed' or else the Prime Minister would campaign to leave the EU meant that either the EU institutions and Member States had to respond immediately or face the consequences. The choice, to respond immediately and agree a deal by 19 February 2016 irrespective of the consequences for rule of law (see discussion below), now seems somewhat quixotic as the British Prime Minister was unable to deliver.

Negotiations within any system of law are subject to the control of the rule of law applicable to that system barring very limited exceptions which are cut out for national security purposes. Inverting the relationship of the norm and exception which is inherent in the Gove argument is an aberration. But not only is it an aberration it is also an insult of substantial proportions regarding the good faith of the EU as a whole. Underlying the argument that no deal could be binding if subject to judicial scrutiny, the UK Justice Minister effectively denounced the rule of law, the capacity of all the 27 Member States to act in accordance with EU law and the principle of legality as a norm in EU law itself. Somewhat

---

15   http://www.consilium.europa.eu/en/press/press-releases/2016/02/02-letter-tusk-proposal-new-settlement-uk/ visited 12 August 2016.

16   http://www.mirror.co.uk/news/uk-news/david-camerons-eu-deal-legally-7429422 visited 5 September 2016.

surprisingly, the Gove attack was taken very seriously in EU circles, no doubt because it received substantial support within the British Government, more widely than just in the Ministry of Justice. The Gove position required the EU to abandon rule of law in respect of its negotiations with the UK and to find an alternative framework within which to conduct the negotiations which would not be subject to EU judicial oversight.[17]

The second victim of the 'speed' imperative was democracy. I will set out below the EU rules for Treaty amendment (which the UK demands would entail). By seeking to transform the deal from one of EU law into one of international law, the parties colluded in the total exclusion of national parliaments, notwithstanding the UK Prime Minister's demand that national parliaments should have more power in the EU system. In this deal, there was no opportunity at all for them to comment formally. Further, national governments were extremely limited in their participation – a mere yes or no in the Council was sufficient for the deal to be done. This yes or no of the Member States was, apparently not even necessary in written form – according to the Opinion of the Legal Service which I will discuss at greater length below,[18] paragraph 5 states "the draft Decision…does not require any formality for the parties to express their consent to be bound. It does not require any formality such as signing or notification of having accomplished a formal ratification or any other procedure in accordance with constitutional requirements." This means that national governments can also be excluded from any discussion of the draft Decision – the Head of State or Government could just nod his or her head and it is a done deal. As no formal ratification procedure in accordance with national law was required, no one needed to be consulted. The European Parliament was also excluded from the negotiations as there was no place for it in the decision of the Heads of State or Government. The purported act of assent of a Head of State of Government might have been unlawful according to any number of national constitutions but that was to be a matter internal to those Member States which could not affect the validity of the act itself. This was the explicit incitement of Heads of State and Governments to act contrary to their national constitutions (all of which have formal rules for the ratification

---

17   It is worth noting as set out above that the UK Government was required to accept judicial oversight of the legality of the Referendum Act as regards who had the right to vote, an issue determined by the (UK) Supreme Court.

18   Council Document 15/16.

of international agreements – assuming as the Council Legal Service does that this is an international agreement).

The third victim of the draft Decision was the courts. As a decision which would be both legal and simultaneously not really legal, the effect was to limit as far as possible the basis for legal challenge before any court, and most importantly the CJEU.

Finally, the Commission, as guardian of the Treaties, was not an innocent bystander in this massacre of EU constitutionality. Not only did it fail to object to the procedure but it tacitly approved it by participating in the design of the draft Decision. It colluded in the pre-emption of EU legality by formally accepting that in the event of the draft Decision coming into effect it would make findings of fact in favour of the UK's demands, which findings of fact would require a consideration of the facts at the time of adoption. This is a pathetic act by the body established with the duty to protect the Treaties and EU legality.

Why did all these institutions and Heads of State and Government behave in such an astonishing manner? The only issue at stake was UK membership of the EU – yet the way in which the UK wielded the threat of departure and terrified the institutions and Heads of State and Government is a salutary tale in international politics. Using the argument of the exceptional need for speed which was completely arbitrary as the UK authorities themselves were entitled to choose the date for the referendum, the UK negotiators pushed their EU counterparts to enter into a deal monstrous in form and content. What was the fear that drove this discussion? Clearly everyone actually engaged in it was convinced that the content of the draft Decision would not pass democratic or judicial scrutiny either at the EU level or at the national level. If the rules were obeyed as set out in the Treaties, there would be no deal of the kind which the British Prime Minister claimed he needed in order to agree to campaign for the UK remain a Member State. So, democracy, legality and legitimacy were dumped in the trash bin in favour of the most autocratic and arbitrary action by Heads of State and Governments.

As if waking up after a night of carnage, the President of the Council, the President of the European Parliament and the Prime Minister of the Member State holding the Presidency of the EU made a joint statement on 24 June 2016, the day after the referendum which included the following:

As agreed, the "New Settlement for the United Kingdom within the European Union", reached at the European Council on 18-19 February 2016, will now not take effect and ceases to exist. There will be no renegotiation."[19] Does one detect a note of humility in this statement? The vehemence of the statements by all the EU institutions and many Heads of State and Government over the weeks following the referendum result that the will of the British people must be respected also perhaps reveals the shame which their own actions have brought to the international stage. As the Presidents of the Council, European Parliament and the Prime Minister of the Presidency stated in their press release of 24 June "We now expect the United Kingdom government to give effect to this decision of the British people as soon as possible, however painful that process may be." On 24 June 2016, everyone wanted to forget and put behind them their own acts of cowardice before the UK Prime Minister's threats.

What are the 'Normal' Rules for Amending EU Law?

Two kinds of amendments to EU legislation would have been required by the draft Decision – first changes to the EU Treaties themselves and secondly the amendment of secondary legislation.

The 2009 Lisbon Treaty amendments to the Treaties set out the rules for amendment in Article 48 TEU, which the UK demands and the response of the Council President would require. There are two procedures – one ordinary the other a simplified revision procedure. According to the ordinary procedure, the Government of any Member State, the European Parliament or the Commission may submit to the Council proposals for amendments. These amendments can either increase or reduce the competences conferred on the Union.[20] National Parliaments must be notified. After consultation with the European Parliament and the Commission the European Council may adopt a decision by simple majority in favour of examining the proposed amendments. The Council President must then convene a Convention composed of representatives

---

19   http://www.consilium.europa.eu/en/press/press-releases/2016/06/24-joint-state-
      ment-uk-referendum/ visited 14 August 2016.

20   An explanation of the separate responsibilities of the Council and the European
      Council in the procedure are not necessary for my purposes.

of the national Parliaments, the Heads of State or Government of the Member States, the European Parliament and the Commission.[21]

It is then for the Convention to examine the proposals for amendment and adopt by consensus a recommendation for a conference of representatives of the governments of the Member States charged with determining, by common accord, the proposed amendments. Any amendment can only enter into force after being ratified by all Member States in accordance with their respective constitutional requirements.[22] The European Council may, however, decide by simple majority with the consent of the European Parliament not to convene a Convention if the extent of the proposed amendments does not justify this. In such a case it is for the European Council to define the terms of reference for a conference of representatives of the governments of the Member States.

The simplified revision procedure commences with a proposal by any of the same parties entitled to invoke the procedure for revision of all or part of the provisions of Part 3 TFEU (the substantive part of EU law including everything from the internal market to tourism and administrative cooperation) relating to internal policies and actions of the Union. The Council is entitled to adopt a decision amending anything in Part 3 by unanimity after consulting the European Parliament and the Commission, and in the case of institutional changes to the monetary area, the European Central Bank. The decision cannot enter into force until it has been approved by the Member States in accordance with their respective constitutional requirements. This procedure cannot be used to increase to EU's competences.[23] Provision is made for notification of national Parliaments but the consent of the European Parliament is required for any substantive amendment and the Council must act by unanimity.

Treaty amendment has been the subject of considerable judicial consideration by the CJEU which has confirmed that this can only take place by means of the amendment procedure currently contained in Article

---

21   In the event of proposed institutional changes in the monetary area the European Central Bank must also be consulted – arguably the case in respect of the British demands regarding the relation of non-Eurozone countries with the Eurozone.

22   Article 48(5) TEU provides that if four fifths of the Member States have ratified the amendments within two years of signature of the treaty providing for them, but one or more Member State is encountering difficulties the matter will be referred to the Council.

23   A few shortcuts are permitted in that in some cases the Council can decide to act by qualified majority or invoke the ordinary legislative procedure where a special one applies according to the TFEU.

48 TEU.[24] It has also confirmed that international agreements which are within the competence of the EU must be entered into in accordance with the procedures set out in the Treaty.

The second type of amendment which the draft Decision would require was to EU secondary legislation. Within the ordinary legislative procedure, what would have applied to all the promises for change in respect of EU citizens, it is for the Commission to propose amendments to legislation and for the Council and European Parliament to adopt them.

Did the Proposed Draft Council DecisionFulfil the Requirements of EU Law?

On 8 February 2016, the Legal Service of the European Council issued an opinion concerning the new settlement with the UK.[25] The opinion deals with the form, legal nature and legal effects of the draft Decision confirming answers given (orally) at the meeting by the EU Council's Legal Counsel on 5 February. First, the legal opinion states that the draft Decision "takes the form of a draft 'Decision of the Heads of State or Government, meeting within the European Council'. It is therefore a Decision of the Member States of the European Union, of an intergovernmental nature, not a decision of the European Council as an institution of the European Union under Article 15 TEU, within the meaning of the fourth paragraph of Article 288 TFEU, which would require to be based on a specific legal basis." The Legal Service avoided altogether any mention of Article 48 TEU which is the mechanism for Treaty amendment, a surprising oversight for such a knowledgeable body. The choice means that effectively the deal would have no legal basis in EU law at all. This is perhaps counterintuitive to the Gove position as it means that instead of the proposed Decision being binding in EU law it would be binding only in the more nebulous world of international law and thus enforcement would be more precarious.

The Council Legal Service's Opinion continues to excuse the use of the phrase "meeting within the European Council" in the heading of the draft Decision as without actual content. The Opinion states that the phrase "'meeting within the European Council' aims only at clarifying that the Heads of State or Government took the opportunity of their participation

---

24   Case 43/75 *Defrenne* ECR [1976] 455; C-68/86 *UK v Council* ECR [1988] 855; C-28/12 *Commission v Council* 29 June 2015.

25   Council Document 15/16.

in a meeting of the European Council, of which they are all members, to adopt their decision." Such a position is odd indeed. If generalised, this would mean that any decision adopted within an EU governance venue could be, at the will of the parties, no longer an EU decision binding the parties within EU law but a private agreement among the parties outside EU law notwithstanding the reference to the EU venue in which it was adopted. The Legal Service supported this interpretation of the draft Decision (not even yet adopted) by making reference to two other circumstances where the Heads of State had adopted such declarations outside the Treaty system. The first circumstance which the Legal Service refers to is the so called Edinburgh Decision of the Council of 12 December 1992. The Danish people had rejected the Maastricht Treaty in a referendum in 1992. The Danish Government considered that the key issue of concern to the Danish people in respect of this negative vote was the creation of EU citizenship. It requested a binding decision of the Council (in accordance with the pre-Maastricht procedures) to be attached to the Treaty confirming that EU citizenship would not replace nationality of a Member State. The decision was adopted as a declaration to the Maastricht Treaty.

The second example to which the Legal Service makes reference is the Decision of the Heads of State or Government of the 27 Member States... on the concerns of the Irish people on the Treaty of Lisbon 19 June 2009. The Irish constitution required a positive vote in referendum of the people to amendment of the EU treaties. In a referendum held in June 2008, the Irish voters rejected the Lisbon Treaty. To address the concerns of the Irish people and pave the way for a new referendum, the Council adopted conclusions including a declaration on workers' rights.[26] The decision was adopted by the Council as such, the European Parliament debated and voted on the inclusion of the declaration as an inherent part of the Lisbon Treaty. The mechanism, a pre-Lisbon one, sought to avoid the need for a full convention of all the Member States to make a minor amendment to the Lisbon Treaty of concern only to one Member State and to pave the way for a new referendum (in which the Irish voters accepted the new Treaty).[27]

---

26   http://ec.europa.eu/dorie/fileDownload.do;jsessionid=pG4MVinW1P7zHkfrf6lQQ Z5NLDhpljPJpvQCfDv5xQ6hvN3lyqLl!-66474968?docId=1485126&cardId=1485125 visited 12 August 2016.

27   Pech, Laurent 'The European Union's Lisbon Treaty: Some Thoughts on the 'Irish Legal Guarantees'" http://www.ejiltalk.org/the-european-unions-lisbon-treaty-some-thoughts-on-the-irish-legal-guarantees/ visited 12 August 2016.

In both the examples provided by the Council's Legal Service, an accommodation was proposed to deal with a specific issue arising in the ratification of Treaty changes which would avoid the need to convoke a full convention of the Member States to consider the addition of a declaration to a Treaty in the process of ratification which had already been ratified by a number of Member States before the issue arose. The specific accommodation in both cases engaged only the one Member State in which the problem arose and would not have consequences for any other Member State. Already in the second case, the European Parliament was fully informed and in due course, accepted the procedure on 18 April 2012.[28]

The next paragraph of the Legal Service's Opinion belies the first argument – it states that the draft Decision is an instrument of international law by which the 28 Member States agree on a joint interpretation of certain provisions of the EU Treaties and on principles and arrangements for action in related circumstances. So far from affecting only one Member State as in the Danish and Irish cases, this Decision would affect everyone and every Member State. The Legal Service makes a series of convoluted arguments about the legality of the draft Decision in international law which has also been the subject of detailed analysis by Dashwood[29] in support of the legally binding nature of the draft Decision and a blistering negative argument by Peers.[30] Personally I find the arguments which Peers puts forward particularly cogent but my purpose here is not to examine the legality of the draft Decision which is disputed not so much in international law as such but in EU law. Instead I would like here to examine what the deal meant in respect of who gets to decide what EU law is.

There are two things which are particularly clear from the Legal Service's note on the draft Decision: first the effect of this troubling approach to amending the treaties is to place the Heads of State and the Governments of the Member States in the driving seat. The draft Decision, in the form of an international agreement means that none of the other EU institutions such as the European Parliament, the Commission and

---

28   http://ec.europa.eu/dorie/fileDownload.do;jsessionid=pG4MV1nW1P7zHkfrf6lQQ
      Z5NLDhpljPJpvQCfDv5xQ6hvN3lyqLl!-66474968?docId=1485126&cardId=1485125
      visited 12 August 2016.

29   https://www.theguardian.com/commentisfree/2016/feb/25/michael-gove-wrong-
      cameron-eu-agreement-legally-binding-european-union-law   visited   13   August
      2016.

30   http://eulawanalysis.blogspot.fr/2016/02/the-draft-ukeu-renegotiation-deal-is-it.
      html visited 13 August 2016.

the European Central Bank have to be consulted or are entitled to give or withhold their consent. Further the CJEU is intended to be excluded from determining the legality of the Decision. The principles of separation of powers which are spelt out clearly in the TEU are circumvented in favour of state sovereignty in its most red-in-tooth-and-claw form. Secondly, as the Legal Service states at paragraph 5 of the Opinion, "It does not require any formality for the parties to express their consent to be bound. It does not require any formality such as signing or notification of having accomplished a formal ratification or another procedure in accordance with constitutional requirements." What the Legal Service seems to be stating is that the draft Decision not only overrides democratic accountability in the EU but also releases the Member States from their national constitutional requirements.[31] So a draft Decision by the Heads of State and Government of the Member States of the EU which would have dramatic consequences for citizens of the Union (see later sections) would not be subject to democratic control at the EU level in the form of the Article 48 TEU carefully crafted provisions and it would also release the Member States from their national constitutional requirements. A stroke of the pen of a Head of State alone would extinguish the rights of millions of EU citizens.

Such an arrangement is monstrous in that it not only deforms both democracy and rule of law in the EU but also purports to deform it in all 28 Member States.

The Council Negotiations

The UK Prime Minister submitted his letter of demands on 10 November 2015 and the President of the Council reported to the Member States by letter on 7 December 2015. According to President Tusk's letter in less than four weeks with the Christmas holidays approaching rapidly (and a change of the Presidency of the EU) he had, in close cooperation with the Commission "held extensive bilateral consultations at Sherpa level with all Member States. We also discussed [the UK demands] with representatives of the European Parliament."[32]

---

31   For an interesting reflection on this aspect of EU administrative law see Harlow, Carol. "Editorial: Transparency, Accountability and the Privileges of Power." *European Law Journal* 22.3 (2016): 273-278.

32   Council Press Release 898/15.

All four areas of demand are dealt with in the letter. On three areas, the Eurozone outs and a right to veto, competitiveness and sovereignty the President affirmed that substantial progress had been made and implicitly the letter appears to suggest that the Council President would be recommending acceptance of the UK demands (which was what happened). On the fourth issue, the rights of EU citizens, there was less agreement. While some issues such as the UK demands on fighting 'abuse' of EU free movement rights and to be relieved of the obligation to pay child benefit to EU citizen workers whose children live in another Member State were resolvable, the issue of equality of EU citizens was still a sticking point. The UK Prime Minister had demanded the right to treat non-British EU citizens as second class, with no right to in-work social benefits until they had lived and worked in the UK for four years. I will come back to the content of the demands and their treatment in a later section. Suffice it here to note that the President of the Council advised the Member States and institutions that equality of EU citizens was still an issue to be resolved. He informed his interlocutors that he would need more time (not surprising as so far he had had less than four weeks) for the precise drafting and legal form (see above).

The President of the Council ended his letter with a warning to everyone: "All involved must take their part of responsibility. I will act as an honest broker but all Member States and the institutions must show readiness for compromise for this process to succeed. Our goal is to find solutions that will meet the expectations of the British Prime Minister, while cementing the foundations on which the EU is based." It would seem that he was already playing into the exceptionalism-speed game which the British Prime Minister sought to impose on the negotiations from the beginning. The President continued "In times when geopolitics is back in Europe, we need to be united and strong." One might well inquire how the EU can be strong and united if it does not respect its own rules and constitutional requirements. Nothing can be more divisive than trying to play by the rules when someone else is cheating. Encouraging the institutions and the Member States to break their rules both EU and national is no way towards unity and strength.

The European Parliament

The 7 December 2015 letter from the President of the Council does not specify with whom he and his team had been in contact at the European

Parliament. In his letter to the Council and institutions of 2 February 2016 where he sets out the draft Decision and supporting documents[33] he makes no reference to the European Parliament. The European Parliament made no press release on the subject of the UK referendum or the negotiations until it held a debate on the subject on 27 June 2016, after the event.[34] The President of the European Parliament addressed the European Parliament once, on 18 February on the subject of the EU referendum.[35] Helpfully, the European Parliamentary Research Service issued an in-depth analysis in February 2016 entitled *The UK's 'new settlement' in the European Union*. The analysis comes from the Members' Research Service and expresses the views of the authors only.[36]

According to this source, the European Parliament's Committee on Constitutional Affairs visited London on 16-17 November 2015 to discuss the referendum. They met with ministers, committees of the two Houses of Parliament, representatives of the political parties, civil society organisations and think tanks. Subsequently, two meetings with President Tusk's negotiating team were held in February 2016. Three MEPs were delegated to these meetings: Elmar Brok (European Peoples Party, Germany), Roberto Gualtieri (Socialist, Italy) and Guy Verhofstadt (Alliance of Liberals and Democrats, Belgium) and one further meeting on 10 February took place with the European Parliament's President, Martin Schultz.

The British Prime Minister met with the leaders of the main European Parliament political parties on 16 February before the Council meeting at which the draft Decision was adopted. The President of the European Parliament addressed the Parliament on 18 February, the day before the Council adopted the draft Decision, on the UK referendum.[37] He ex-

---

33   Council Press Release 23/16.

34   http://www.europarl.europa.eu/news/en/news-room/plenary/2016-06-28/1 visited 14 August 2016.

35   http://www.europarl.europa.eu/the-president/en/press/press_release_speeches/speeches/speeches-2016/speeches-2016-february/pdf/speech-at-the-european-council-by-martin-schulz-president-of-the-european-parliament visited 14 August 2016.

36   Poptcheva, E-M and D Eatock *The UK's 'new' settlement' in the European Union* EPRS PE 577.983. Pages 22-23 deal with the role of the European Parliament in the negotiations.

37   http://www.europarl.europa.eu/the-president/en/press/press_release_speeches/speeches/speeches-2016/speeches-2016-february/pdf/speech-at-the-european-council-by-martin-schulz-president-of-the-european-parliament visited 14 August 2016.

pressed his support for the UK's continuing membership of the EU and stated that this was the wish of the overwhelming majority of the MEPs. But he criticised the proposed draft Decision on every ground. First, he expressed the European Parliament's strong support for the 'ever closer union' of the EU as the way forward. He supported the Euro, warning that it is the currency of the EU and the UK has no more than an opt out. Regarding EU citizens, the President criticised the draft decision which would have created discrimination among EU citizens in the field of pay and working conditions. He stated "Allow me to say this very clearly: The European Parliament will fight against discrimination between EU citizens. Non-discrimination and equal treatment are fundamental principles of our Union."

Further and perhaps most importantly, on the legality of the draft Decision mechanism, the President brought legality back into the debate: "We welcome the fact that the ordinary legislative procedure is the one proposed but you will surely understand that no parliament in the world can prejudge the outcome of its legislative work." Yet, the European Parliament's President also took part in the Council meeting on 19 February when the draft Decision was adopted.

Returning to the in-depth analysis of the European Parliamentary Research Service, in the event of the draft Decision becoming effective (after a UK vote to remain in the EU) the European Parliament would be co-legislator with the Council on amendment of any secondary legislation foreseen by the Decision. This would mean that the European Parliament would be able to block the promised changes if it so voted. This position is quite different from that adopted by the Commission which I will deal with in the next section. Finally, the European Parliament would be represented in any Convention established under Article 48 TEU to amend the treaties. The analysis in the in-depth note appears to be that although the draft Decision purports to bind all parties in international law to carry out specific treaty amendments, when and if the time came to actually implement the Decision, the European Parliament would not be bound by that Decision. In the convention which would have to be convoked, the participating members of the European Parliament would not be bound by the political Decision.

One cannot say that the European Parliament covered itself in glory in upholding the rule of law and challenging the purported exercise of arbitrary state sovereignty, but at least it did not participate actively in promoting the deformation of rule of law and democracy. Whether it should have used its legislative powers more vigorously to stop the monstrous process which was under way and undermining democracy and rule of law in the EU is another matter.

The European Commission

The specific task of the European Commission is to be the guardian of the EU Treaties. It has the exclusive right of initiative to propose EU legislation (with minor exceptions which do not apply to the fields relevant here). It also oversees the implementation of EU law according to the interpretation given to EU law by the CJEU which has the monopoly over the correct interpretation of EU law. According to the Commission's website "It acts in the EU's general interest with complete independence from national governments and is accountable to the European Parliament."[38] A number of the promises of the draft Decision of the Council would require the Commission to make proposals for new legislation. The Presidency Conclusions which contain the draft Decision, now entitled the New Settlement for the United Kingdom in the European Union, would become effective on the date the UK informed the Secretary-General of the Council that the United Kingdom has decided to remain a member of the European Union. Nonetheless, the agreement on the draft Decision was specifically stated to be legal binding in international law. The document is set out in seven Annexes. The first contains the Decision of the Heads of State or Government concerning the new settlement for the UK. Annexes II and III deal with the banking Union issues and competitiveness. Annex IV contains measures on a subsidiarity implementation mechanism and a burden reduction implementation mechanism. Annexes V – VII contain declarations by the Commission of the actions it would take in the event of the entry into force of the Decision.

Annex V contains an undertaking by the Commission to make a proposal for amendment of the EU's regulation on coordination of social security (Regulation 883/2004) to deal with child benefit demands of the UK (but which would be applicable to all Member States). Annex VI is more problematic. Here the Commission promises to propose an amendment to the regulation on free movement of workers (Regulation 493/2011) to insert a safeguard mechanism which could be used by the UK to limit or prevent free movement of workers to the UK from other

---

38   http://eur-lex.europa.eu/summary/glossary/european_commission.html visited 15 August 2016.

Member States.[39] It is problematic that the Commission should propose an amendment to secondary legislation which would effectively limit one of the four freedoms which constitute the internal market. Such an undertaking raises questions about the independence of the Commission and its fulfilment of its role as guardian of the Treaties. The Commission's declaration specifically states that it is designed to 'act as a solution' to the UK's concerns about inflows of workers, thus an act to address a complaint of one Member State only and a complaint, the accuracy of which was much debated by experts. The Commission then states in its declaration that it will accept the information provided by the UK on free movement of workers of other Member States to the UK as showing that the exceptional situation which would be provided for in the proposed safeguard provision (tacitly assuming that it would be adopted by the Council and the European Parliament in the form proposed by the Commission) exists. Thus on 19 February 2016, the Commission declares that the UK will "be justified in triggering the mechanism in the full expectation of obtaining approval" sometime after 23 June 2016 (the referendum date).

This declaration purports to bind the Commission to accept on the basis of past information and with no revised and updated evaluation of the actual situation at the time that the proposed mechanism might be triggered, the UK's entitlement to prevent free movement of workers from other Member States to the UK. The Commission binds itself to an assurance to the UK that it could rely on the approval of the Commission at that future date without demure. The monstrousness of this assurance is astonishing. The Commission appears to be willing to throw the whole rule book of rule of law and the primacy of the internal market into the trash bin.

The next annex, VII, also contains a declaration of the Commission. This one relates to issues related to the abuse of the right of free movement of persons. I will return in a later section to the content of the declaration but here I will deal with the constitutionality of the contents of the declaration. The Commission undertakes to adopt a text which it describes as a 'proposal' which would complement the directive on the rights of EU citizens and their family members in two main ways,

---

39   The exact wording is: "a safeguard mechanism with the understanding that it can and will be used and therefore will act as a solution to the United Kingdom's concerns about the exceptional inflow of workers from elsewhere in the European Union that it has seen over the last years."

allowing Member States to exclude from the scope of the directive third country national family members who have not been authorised to enter the host Member State and exclude from the directive (and effectively the Treaties) EU citizens returning to their home state after residing in a host Member State from taking their third country national family members home with them. Both these issues have been considered (more than once) by the CJEU and its constant jurisprudence is clear, precise and unconditional – Member States cannot make family reunion with third country national family members subject to national immigration rules.[40] The entitlement of EU citizens returning to their home Member State taking their third country national family members with them has also been determine clearly and precisely by the CJEU in favour of this right.[41] None of this jurisprudence is new but follows a continuous line of decisions from the early 1990s. That the Commission, as guardian of the Treaties consistent with the interpretation given to them by the CJEU, should undertake such obvious disobedience to the constitutional structure of the EU is indeed shocking.

The undertakings of the Commission in the context of the New Settlement for the UK with the EU are not only inconsistent with the Treaties and the EU's secondary legislation but a direct challenge to the monopoly of the CJEU to interpret the Treaties and secondary legislation. These actions have the effect of weakening and diminishing not only the authority of the Commission but the whole of the EU.

Conclusions

The negotiations between the UK and the EU institutions which gave rise to the draft Decision on the New Settlement for the UK in the EU provide a textbook example of how not to do things. The UK Prime Minister in his demands revealed the UK as arrogant, unreasonable and unreliable. Further events proved the Prime Minister ineffective and unable to deliver on his promises. The documents indicate that the UK government was content to bully all the institutions and Member States, manufacturing imperatives both as regards speed and content of a deal which were utterly self serving and had the conspicuous effect of preventing any reasonable discussion of the demands.

---

40   C-127/08 *Metock* [2008] ECR I-6241.
41   C-456/12 *O* 12 March 2014; C-457/12 *S* 12 March 2014.

The EU institutions, but most specifically the Council and the Commission betrayed their duties to act in good faith in the best interests of the Union and as guarantors of the treaties. In their eagerness to accommodate the UK demands, they revealed utter contempt for the rights of EU citizens. Even the rights of EU citizens most deeply embedded in the treaties, the subject of extensive jurisprudence over forty years were cast aside by these actors in their efforts to appease the British negotiators. The Commission went even further and betrayed the CJEU and its constant jurisprudence in its efforts. And all of this for nothing – the UK Prime Minister was unable to deliver but the EU was seriously weakened as both an Internal Market and an Area of Freedom, Security and Justice.

Monstrous Citizenships

Arguing with the past, like paying taxes, like observing the law,
like queuing, like not playing music full blast when others will
be disturbed, has suddenly become a vital part of being a member
of society, an ordinary but important act of citizenship,
a factor in establishing the idea of home as a place
you would like to belong and might be allowed to stay.

> MARINA WARNER *Managing Monsters: Six Myths of Our Times – The Reith*
> *Lectures 1994*

Introduction

One consequence of the UK vote to leave the EU is that the approximately 65 million British citizens living anywhere in the world (though most of them live in the UK) will cease to be citizens of the European Union. The nationals of the other 27 Member States (about 445 million of them) will continue to be citizens of the European Union. Some of those British citizens may have acquired citizenship of another Member State and so will remain EU citizens notwithstanding. Some nationals of the 27 other Member States will also have acquired British citizenship but retained their previous nationality and through it, EU citizenship. BREXIT will be the biggest bonfire of citizenship status in UK law since the independence of the colonies in the 20th century when nationals of the (then) newly independent states lost their status as British.[1]

From 24 June 2016, the day following the referendum vote, there has been an explosion of racially motivated attacks in the UK. The Institute of Race Relations has opened a special webpage compiling news reports of these attacks.[2] Many attacks have been directed against EU citizens from other Member States and were clearly well organised[3] others have been

---

[1]   This history is complex and the change of titles from British subject, citizenship of the UK and colonies to British citizenship in 1981 papers over an astonishing number of injustices some of which I will return to later. Dummett, Ann. *The Acquisition of British Citizenship. From Imperial Traditions to National Definitions.* na, 1994.

[2]   http://www.irr.org.uk/news/post-brexit-racism/ visited 21 August 2016.

[3]   24 June: Laminated cards are left at schools and homes In Huntingdon, Cambridgeshire, with the words 'No more Polish Vermin' in English and Polish. An

directed at British citizens of visible ethnic minorities[4] and there is no sign of these attacks letting up. They have been deplored by the (former and current) British Prime Ministers and many antiracism organisations. A new chair of the Equality and Human Rights Commission (EHRC) was appointed at the end of April 2016. In a wide ranging EHRC report issued on 18 August 2016 he stated "The combination of the post-BREXIT rise in hate crimes and deep race inequality in Britain is very worrying and must be tackled urgently."[5] The vote to cease to be EU citizens appears to have opened the gates of racism long embedded in the British debates about who are 'really' British. A part of the British public appears to have considered the referendum a vote on who should not be British because they do not 'belong' in the UK. This question of belonging will become a central element in this section.

What is the most important difference between British citizenship and EU citizenship – what is it that the British voters have decided they no longer want? In my opinion there is one crucial difference between the two – rights. British citizenship is not based on rights, there is no bill of rights, there is no written constitution and rights attaching to British citizenship seem to come primarily from international law. I will develop on this below. EU citizenship is created by a treaty (currently the TFEU) and is based on specific and stated rights. The contours of those rights have been the matter of much judicial consideration and I will return to this as well further on in this section.

The 20th century debate in the UK about British citizenship weaves a drunken path about how to define who is 'really' one of us and who is not 'really' and so should not be citizens. This debate would fuel the actions of successive British Governments through the period of independence of the colonies but it would also haunt the residents of the British isles up to the current day. This debate is curiously detached from any debate about the entitlement of citizens to have rights. Instead it tends to turn into a dog whistle for ethnic division, discrimination and racism.

11-year-old boy who finds one of the cards says he feels 'really sad'. (BBC News, 27 June 2016 and Cambridge News, 26 June 2016).

4   24 June: Caerphilly born Shazia Awan, a Remain campaigner, is told to 'pack her bag and go home' on Twitter. (*Independent*, 25 June 2016).

5   https://www.equalityhumanrights.com/en visited 21 August 2016.

British Citizenship and Rights

In July 2007 the then (Labour) Government issued a Command Paper entitled *The Governance of Britain*.[6] In section 4 the document examines Britain's future: the citizen and the state. It provides an excellent starting point for my investigation into British citizenship and rights as little has actually changed in legal or practical terms since this overview except to make British citizenship even more precarious. The document commences with recognition that the right to citizenship in law comes from the rules of British nationality (para 180) but immediately moves to the question of identity and multiple identities (paras 181-2). It suggests that British citizenship should be an overarching status to which the common factor is national identity. It recommends that we look to history to help define citizenship acknowledging that there is a relative lack of precision about what it means to be British (para 184). The document proposes that many cultural traits and traditions are distinctively British (para 185) and provide a basis for identity. But it considers that the rights and responsibilities that accompany British citizenship need to be meaningful for two groups – new arrivals and young people. It recognises that entitlement to rights often considered inherent in citizenship such as voting and standing for election are not aligned to British citizenship (para 192). British citizens are deprived of voting rights after 15 years absences from the UK while Irish nationals and Commonwealth citizens (including Cypriots and Maltese EU citizens) resident in the UK are entitled to do both. Rather bizarrely, the document states "A number of rights stem from EU citizenship but few if any are available uniquely to British citizens" (para 192). Do we detect here a hankering for an EU citizenship which provides rights *only* for British citizen not to nationals of the other 27 Member States? I will discuss below the issue of EU citizenship and rights but already in this document it is clear that rights for all EU citizens rather than just for British citizens rankles.

The document moves immediately to the issue of what it terms 'potential citizens' – a clear signpost that what is under discussion is immigration. Why does any discussion about British citizenship move so quickly from identity to migration and particularly immigration? Perhaps the reason is to be found in the content of rights. According to the long standing approach of British jurists to examine an issue from the perspective

6   https://www.gov.uk/government/uploads/system/uploads/attachment_data/
     file/228834/7170.pdf visited 21 August 2016.

of history, a 2015 Supreme Court judgment on deprivation of British citizenship (to which I will return shortly)[7] digs about in Blackstone's *Commentaries on the Laws of England* 15th edition 1809 (Vol 1 p 137) to discover what right attaches to being British (para 97). The Supreme Court confirms the view that a British subject enjoys a constitutional right to reside in or return to that part of the Queen's dominions of which he or she is a citizen. The language of subjects and dominions is that of colonialism where the British Government claimed the right to tell British subjects in which bits of the Empire they were entitled to live (and *a contrario* where they should not be). But leaving the colonial history aside, what is somewhat surprising is that the first and perhaps only true right attached to British citizenship is to enter and reside in the UK. This means that the fundamental purpose of British citizenship, as far as rights are concerned, is immigration related. Perhaps then it is not so surprising that at least some of those who voted to leave the EU in the referendum transposed that vote into one of immigration, if that is indeed the core of what it means to be British.

The 2007 Government document examining governance in Britain focuses on only two groups – those who seek to become British citizens and young people. As far as immigrants are concerned, the document suggests that "an approach which offered genuine benefits to permanent residents could offer greater transparency and credibility and encourage new citizens to integrate into wider British society, helping them participate in our democracy." But the document then states that the measures which the Government has taken to raise the profile and meaning of citizenship are the introduction of a language test and a multiple choice test entitled Knowledge of Life (in the UK) for permanent residents seeking to naturalise as British. So the meaning of British citizenship seems to be intrinsically bound to how difficult it is to obtain. It it not related to rights (or even duties) but to the ability of those seeking it to pass tests (which of course privileges the well educated who have already demonstrated their capacity to pass tests).[8] The policy proposal of the document for a more meaningful British citizenship addressed those seeking to acquire British citizenship. In addition to passing tests, proving financial solvency and good character, they would also be required to carry out voluntary work in the interest of social cohesion to gain necessary credits

---

7   *Pham v Secretary of State for the Home Department* [2015] UKSC 19.

8   Ryan, Bernard F. «Integration requirements: A new model in migration law.» (2008).

to naturalise.[9] The emphasis is entirely on how to demarcate the line between those who are immigrants and those who are citizens by making that line more difficult and complex to cross. More people would remain immigrants and only the well educated with time to do voluntary work would become citizens. The British discussion of rights and obligations of citizenship is fixated on one right only – the right to live in the UK. When the Government changed after elections in 2010, the proposals on 'earned' citizenship were dropped.[10]

The singularity of the one right of British citizenship – the right to enter and reside in the UK – has been grudgingly recognised by the UK Government though sometimes denied. The UK Government has never ratified Protocol 4 of the European Convention of Human Rights which includes the right of citizens to enter and reside in their country.[11] It signed the protocol on the date when it was opened for signature 16 September 1963 but never ratified it. Examining the UK's commitments under the European Convention on Human Rights in 2005, the UK Joint Parliamentary Committee on Human Rights which reviewed the Government's report on the ECHR, noted that in relation to Protocol 4 the Government stated its "continuing concerns over Articles 2 and 3 of Protocol 4 which could be taken, respectively, to confer rights in relation to passports and a right of abode on categories of British nationals who do not currently have that right."[12] The 'right of abode' is a UK code term for the right of people in law to enter and reside in the UK. The position has not changed since.

One of the most shameful denials of the relationship of citizenship and the right of residence in the UK dates to the 1960-70 expulsion of East African Asians from Kenya, Uganda and Tanzania (and other East African countries following their independence and the Africanisation policies of the new governments) and the refusal of the UK Government to allow even those with British passports (designating them as citizens of the UK and colonies – the (then) current citizenship status of British citizens) to

---

9   http://image.guardian.co.uk/sys-files/Politics/documents/2008/03/11/citizenship-report-full.pdf visited 21 August 2016.

10   https://www.gov.uk/government/speeches/immigration-home-secretarys-speech-of-5-november-2010 visited 21 August 2016.

11   Article 3(2) Protocol 4 European Convention on Human Rights "No one shall be deprived of the right to enter the territory of the State of which he is a national."

12   http://www.publications.parliament.uk/pa/jt200405/jtselect/jtrights/99/9906.htm visited 21 August 2016.

enter the UK.[13] On independence of these African states, the Asian populations which had by and large moved to them during British rule, were given the choice (by the British authorities) of either becoming citizens of the newly independent states or remaining British. Many of them, Lord Lester estimates about 200,000,[14] elected to remain British as they feared the arrival of Africanisation policies which would require them to leave East Africa. The British Government of the day promised those who chose to remain British that they would always have refuge in the UK. Further, those East African Asians who elected to remain British did not acquire nationality of the newly independent state (where most of them had been born). Sure enough, the Africanisation policies were put into effect in the three countries, the most horrific of which in Uganda, 1972, President Idi Amin threatened to kill any East African Asians who had not left the country within 90 days of his decree.[15] Not surprisingly, many East African Asians with British passports began to arrive in the UK to take refuge in 'their' country anticipating their expulsion.

In three days in February 1968, Parliament adopted the Commonwealth Immigrants Act 1968 (amending an act of the same name of 1962) which had the effect of depriving this group of British nationals of the right of entry and residence in the UK on the basis of their race. This deprivation of the one right which British citizenship is said to provide could not be challenged successfully before the UK courts. A group of the people deprived of their right to enter 'their' country did bring a challenge to the European Court of Human Rights but of course it was not possible to plead a breach of Article 3 Protocol 4 as the UK was not bound by it. Instead the plaintiffs argued that their treatment constituted a breach of Article 3 – inhuman and degrading treatment by reason of racial discrimination (prohibited by Article 14 ECHR). The European Commission of Human Rights agreed with the plaintiffs in its decision of 1973:[16] "The Commission finds it established that the 1968 Act had racial motives and that it covered a racial group. When it was introduced into Parliament as a Bill, it was clear that it was directed against the Asian citizens of

---

13   35 *East African Asians v. the United Kingdom* (application n° 06.03.1978 (decision of the European Commission of Human Rights).

14   Lester, A, *Five Ideas to Fight For* Oneworld, London 2016, pp 67-72.

15   Tandon, Yash. "The expulsions from Uganda: Asians' role in East Africa." *Patterns of Prejudice* 6.6 (1972): 1-8; Patel, Hasu H. "General Amin and the Indian exodus from Uganda." *Issue: A Journal of Opinion* 2.4 (1972): 12-22.

16   *East African Asians v the UK* 4403/70 [1973] ECHR 2 (14 December 1973).

the United Kingdom and Colonies in East Africa and especially those in Kenya. The Commission refers in this connection to statements made in both Houses of Parliament during the debate on the Bill in February 1968." This shameful act by the UK Government has cast a long shadow. By 2001 some rather sophisticated amendments and changes to British nationality law had taken place – most importantly the British Nationality Act 1981 which created British citizenship but deprived quite a number of people who had enjoyed the common status of 'citizen of the UK and colonies' with those who were transitioned into the new British citizenship but were hived off by the legislation into other statuses.

The most unfortunate of this group were those categorised as British Overseas citizens who held limited British passports which gave them the right to live nowhere in the world.[17] This group included most of the East African Asians who had chosen to remain British in the 1960s and 1970s. They had no right to enter the UK but neither did (or does) their status give them the right to live anywhere else in the world.[18] In 2001 an British East African Asian sought to rely on her EU citizenship to enjoy a right to live in the EU (including the UK). Ms Kaur, a British Overseas citizen who had been born in Kenya before independence, sought to use the then fairly new status of citizen of the European Union as a springboard to obtain the right to live in the UK. Her case was referred to the CJEU which found that the UK had a sovereign right to determine who its nationals are for the purposes of EU law (and had not designated British Overseas citizens as such). The CJEU could not go behind this sovereign act.[19] However, in 2015, the UK's Supreme Court when considering the relationship of British citizenship with EU citizenship referred to the decision.[20] The judge who gave the lead opinion, Lord Carnwath, stated "In *Kaur* the applicant was a Kenyan citizen of Asian origin..." (para. 44). I will return below to the *Pham* judgment in more depth. There is no indication in the CJEU *Kaur* judgment or Opinion of the Advocate-General that Ms. Kaur had any citizenship other than British. The assumption was that she was only a British Overseas citizen. So there is nothing sacred about the one Brit-

---

17 MacDonald, Ian Alexander, and Ronan Toal, eds. *Macdonald's Immigration law and practice*. 2015.

18 Goodwin-Gill, Guy S. International Law and the Movement of Persons between States (1978), 212-26; https://www.gov.uk/types-of-british-nationality/british-overseas-citizen visited 21 August 2016.

19 C-192/99 *Kaur* [2001]ECRI-1237.

20 *Pham* [2015]UKSC 19.

ish citizenship right in UK law – it can be transformed when Parliament considers this necessary and the legal and democratic processes of the UK may not correct the injustice. Further, the British Government has no qualms about creating so-called citizenship statuses which lack the essential element of the right to enter and live in one's country. However, the international norm of citizens having the right to enter their country has taken hold in the UK to some extent. This has led an increasingly anxious British Government to provide itself with ever more draconian powers to deprive British citizens of their citizenship altogether. This is a variation on a theme as it means that instead of creating empty citizenships, like British Overseas citizenship, it provides itself with powers to take citizenship away from its citizens thus enabling them to be expelled. In so far as citizenship and the right to enter and reside on the territory of the state have become inextricably linked, the British Government has considered it expedient to have ever greater powers to deprive people of British citizenship.

When some order was introduced into the post-colonial legal order of British-ness, the British Nationality Act 1981 was passed creating a jumble of different classes of British-ness (including British Overseas citizens) but with an implicit subtext that that all but one of them (British citizenship) should eventually cease to exist through the passage of time. A provision of this act allowed the Secretary of State to deprive someone of British citizenship (or one of the other British statuses) on a variety of grounds which were fairly limited. From 2002 onwards these grounds for deprivation of citizenship began to be widened.[21] The first changes were contained in the Nationality, Immigration and Asylum Act 2002. These were followed by more generous provisions for the Secretary of State to deprive people of their citizenship in the Immigration, Asylum and Nationality Act 2006. In particular the Secretary of State was now permitted to take away British citizenship on the ground that this would be conducive to the public good. The Immigration Act 2014 widened, once again, the grounds on which British citizenship could be taken away from anyone (this time including people born such citizens) including if the Secretary of State considered their conduct prejudicial to the vital interests of the UK. A (limited) bar on creating statelessness only applies to those born British not to those naturalised.

---

21   Mantu, Sandra. *Contingent Citizenship: The Law and Practice of Citizenship Deprivation in International, European and National Perspectives*. Brill, 2015.

It is worth pausing briefly to examine the titles of these Acts of Parliament. The title of the first commences with 'Nationality' indicating that these changes to the status of British citizens are an important feature of the Act. The second amending Act in 2006 has a title which indicates that it is about immigration and asylum primarily but adds Nationality as a third sphere of concern. The last Act in 2014, is simply entitled an Immigration Act. No reference is made in the title to its consequences for British citizenship. On the basis of this hierarchy, citizenship slips from a separate domain of legislation in 1981 to a space shared with immigration and asylum in 2002 and finally in 2014 it disappears into the general field of immigration. Legislation which changed profoundly the relationship of the citizen and the state does not even signal in its title that nationality is addressed in it. Symbolically and in the political imagination British citizenship appears to have become only another immigration status which can be gained or lost at the discretion of a Secretary of State.

The right of those born British citizens to their citizenship[22] becomes contingent, as a result of the 2014 Act, on whether or not there are reasonable grounds to consider that the individual could be eligible for another nationality (S 66 Immigration Act 2014). The reasonableness of the grounds are determined by the Secretary of State subject to review by the courts. In light of the title of the Act, one about immigration, the necessity to determine whether an individual in the sights of the Secretary of State for deprivation of citizenship has another citizenship is directly related to where the person can be sent. Anyone who is a naturalised British citizen can be deprived of their British citizenship without any concern as to whether this would render them stateless. If they were born British but the Secretary of State determines that they should no longer be British then the key is what other country can be made responsible for receiving them. Indeed, the Act is about immigration – how to turn citizens into immigrants who can be expelled. This process demands that there be some other country which can be made responsible in nationality law for the individual. Only then can the de-nationalised former British citizen be transformed into a successful immigrant – one who can be expelled somewhere else.

For those British citizens who acquired their citizenship through naturalisation, the 2014 Act no longer requires an examination of whether

---

22   Irrespective of the rights which attach to British citizenship.

they would be stateless as a result of deprivation of British citizenship.[23] According to research carried out by the Bureau of Investigative Journalism[24] since 2010, the British Home Secretary (now Prime Minister) deprived 33 people of British citizenship but did so when most of them were outside the UK so that they cannot come back to the UK even to pursue their appeals against the decision. Immigration related considerations seem to be foremost in decisions about nationality deprivation in the UK. Thus once again it is that one key characteristic of British citizenship – the right to enter and live in the UK – which the British Government considered unacceptable.

As the Home Office (the ministry responsible for citizenship) advised in writing to the Home Affairs Committee of the House of Commons in the context of its inquiry into counter-terrorism, "Deprivation of British citizenship results in simultaneous loss of the right of abode in the United Kingdom and so paves the way for possible immigration detention, deportation or exclusion from the UK."[25]

That British citizens should have any inalienable right appears to be inimical to the British Parliament. This may sound rather exaggerated but the slide away from even the most basic inalienable citizenship right (to enter one's country) has gained momentum. In the Counter-Terrorism and Security Act 2015 Parliament approved new powers for the Secretary of State to exclude British citizens from entering the UK. This new power is entirely consistent with the degradation of citizenship rights which is inherent in British legislation from 2002 onwards. By 2015, Parliament was ready to accept that even British citizenship, however acquired, was no more than an immigration status which could be tampered with at the discretion of the Secretary of State. Legislation passed in 2015 permits the Secretary of State to make a temporary exclusion order against a British citizen otherwise entitled to enter and live in the UK. The ground for such an order is that the Home Secretary 'reasonably suspects' that the person has been involved in terrorism-related activity outside the UK.

---

23   Gower, Melanie. «Deprivation of British citizenship and withdrawal of passport facilities.» *House of Commons Library, SN/HA/6820* (*www. parliament. uk/business/ publications/rese   arch/briefing-papers/SN06820/deprivation-ofbritish-citizenship-and-withdrawal-of-passportfacilities*) (2014).

24   https://www.thebureauinvestigates.com/2016/06/21/citizenship-stripping-new-figures-reveal-theresa-may-deprived-33-individuals-british-citizenship/ visited 22 August 2016.

25   Home Affairs Committee, *Counter-terrorism* 9 May HC 231 of 2013-14.

The consequence of an order is that the individual's travel document is cancelled and the person's name is added to relevant border watch lists.[26] The order lasts for two years unless revoked earlier.[27] In this logic, even British citizens become the responsibility of other countries as regards entry and residence. Temporary exclusion orders take British citizenship law back to 1968. The grudging acceptance by the British Government after the East African Asians scandal that British citizens might have a right to enter and live in the UK is once again disputed.

The relationship of British citizenship and rights is a tenuous one. The central citizenship right in international law – the right to enter and live in your country of nationality – is constantly under scrutiny in the UK. In 1968 the UK Parliament rejected this right for citizens in a highly visible and shocking manner leaving hundreds of thousands of their citizens stranded in countries where their lives were at risk. Under pressure from European human rights law, the UK eventually accepted some (limited) duties towards its citizens enhanced after 1973 (the date of the decision of the European Commission of Human Rights against the UK) but this consensus that citizenship might be more than another immigration status was eroded from 2002 onwards. By 2015 this bonfire of citizenship rights was in full swing and even the right of British citizens to go 'home' was abolished. The objective of the 2015 legislation was to ensure that some British citizens had to stay in foreign countries and could not return to the UK.

Citizenship of the European Union and Rights

The European Union created citizenship of the Union in a flurry of negotiations about treaty changes in 1991.[28] The history has been well researched and written by a number of authors in the field of European

---

26 Gower, Melanie. "Deprivation of British citizenship and withdrawal of passport facilities." *House of Commons Library, SN/HA/6820 (www. parliament. uk/business/publications/research/briefing-papers/SN06820/deprivation-ofbritish-citizenship-and-withdrawal-of-passportfacilities)* (2014).

27 S 4 Counter-Terrorism and Security Act 2015.

28 Article 20 TFEU; Closa, Carlos. "The concept of citizenship in the treaty on European Union." *Common Market Law Review* 29.6 (1992): 1137-1169; Wiener, Antje, and Vincent Della Sala. "Constitution-making and Citizenship Practice–Bridging the Democracy Gap in the EU?." *JCMS: Journal of Common Market Studies* 35.4 (1997): 595-614.

studies.[29] For my purposes it is the relationship of EU citizenship and rights which is of particular interest. The acquisition of EU citizenship is a rather straight forward matter – every national of a Member State is a citizen of the EU. Thus the main way in which citizenship of the Union has been acquired by people has been by the enlargement of the Union – 1994 to Austria and the Nordic states, 2004 to the Baltic, Central and Eastern European states and the two Mediterranean islands, 2007 two more Central European/Balkan countries joined followed by another Balkan country (Croatia) in 2013. Birth rates in all EU countries have been below replacement levels for more than a decade.[30]

Because EU citizenship was created by a treaty, it is based on rights. Article 20(2) TFEU states that citizens shall enjoy the rights and be subject to the duties provided for in the Treaties. The first and most important right is to move and reside freely within the territory of the Member States in conditions of equality with nationals of that state. In the final weeks of the campaign in the UK regarding the referendum on EU membership, this citizenship right – that of nationals of other Member States to move freely to and reside in the UK with equal rights was a matter of intense debate and hostility. Even the House of Commons briefing paper of 29 March 2016 on EU citizens and their right to social benefits describes EU citizens as "EEA migrants".[31] (The EEA is the European Economic Area which includes the Norwegians, Liechtensteiners and Icelanders (the Swiss are covered by other arrangements) and the EU states.) But EU citizens are co-citizens with British citizens. Norwegians, Liechtensteiners and Icelanders have rights as a result of the EEA Agreement between their countries (within the context of the European Free Trade Association) and the EU. The assimilation of EU citizens and their right to move and reside in the UK under conditions of equality in accordance with EU law to 'migrants' evidences a hostility of substantial proportions. Yet this

---

29   Shaw, Jo. "The interpretation of European Union citizenship." *The Modern Law Review* 61.3 (1998): 293-317 ; Bellamy, Richard, and Alex Warleigh-Lack. "From an Ethics of Integration to an Ethics of Participation: Citizenship and the Future of the European Union." *Millennium: A Journal of International Studies* 27 (1998): 447-70.

30   http://ec.europa.eu/eurostat/statistics-explained/index.php/Fertility_statistics The fertility rate in the EU in 2014 was 1.58 children per woman; this was up from the 2001 rate of 1.48 children per woman. 2.1 is the internationally accepted fertility rate for replacement of the population.

31   http://researchbriefings.parliament.uk/ResearchBriefing/Summary/SN04737 visited 22 August 2016.

is the title of an official publication of the UK Parliament issued only a few months before the referendum date.[32]

EU citizens are also entitled to political rights – to vote and stand for election at European Parliament elections and at the municipal level – in any host Member State where they live. They are also entitled to transparency rights and the right of petition to the European Parliament and Ombudsman. However, their political rights do not extend to national elections and on this ground those resident in the UK were excluded from the right to vote in the referendum on EU membership. The right to move and reside was given specific form in secondary legislation by Directive 2004/38.[33] The right is not unqualified – Member States can restrict entry and residence of nationals of other Member States on grounds of public policy, public health and public security. These terms have been much litigated before the CJEU which has provided a restrictive interpretation of them as restrictions on one of the fundamental freedoms of the EU.[34]

Further, from 2000, the EU has a Charter of Fundamental Rights.[35] From the entry into force of the Lisbon Treaty in 2009, the Charter has become legally binding as part of EU law and can be relied upon by anyone within the personal and material scope of EU law.[36] This Charter must be read also as a bill of rights both for EU citizens and for third country nationals living in or affect by EU law. For British citizens, the EU Charter together with the European Convention on Human Rights are the two main sources of human rights in the absence of any national bill of rights. While there has been a substantial debate in the UK that perhaps there needs to be a UK source of rights this has not happened. But this debate

---

32   Wilson, Wendy. "EU migrants: entitlement to housing assistance (England)." *House of Commons Library Standard Note* (2016).

33   Directive 2004/38/EC of the European Parliament and of the Council of 29 April 2004 on the right of citizens of the Union and their family members to move and reside freely within the territory of the Member States amending Regulation (EEC) No 1612/68 and repealing Directives 64/221/EEC, 68/360/EEC, 72/194/EEC, 73/148/ EEC, 75/34/EEC, 75/35/EEC, 90/364/EEC, 90/365/EEC and 93/96/EEC.

34   Bigo, Didier. "Reflections on Immigration Controls and Free Movement in Europe." *Constructing and Imagining Labour Migration: Perspectives of Control from Five Continents* (2016): 293.

35   Peers, Steve, et al., eds. *The EU Charter of fundamental rights: a commentary.* Bloomsbury Publishing, 2014.

36   On the personal and material scope of the Charter see Lenaerts, Koen. "Exploring the limits of the EU Charter of Fundamental Rights." *European Constitutional Law Review* 8.03 (2012): 375-403.

in the UK has been driven by the wish of an influential part of the Conservative Party to repeal legislation which incorporates the ECHR into British law.[37] The proposal for a British Bill of Rights and Responsibilities was to have been published 'shortly' when the Conservative Party issued its document outlining the a new relationship for the UK with human rights in general in 2014.[38] Nothing further has happened.

From its creation, EU citizenship has been an important source of rights for people seeking to establish entitlements in respect of their own governments. I will return to this matter in a later section when I consider 'monstrous families'. Here I will examine only the interpretation of EU citizenship rights as regards the right of citizens to live in their country. Following the 1991 creation of EU citizenship not much happened as regards the clarification of rights for a number of years. I have already mentioned the 2001 *Kaur* decision of the CJEU where it refrained from entering into the UK citizenship debate. However, the first substantive step of the CJEU into the citizenship fray was in 1998 in a decision *Martinez Sala*[39] where the court found that EU citizenship entitled its holders to live in any Member State and to enjoy equal treatment with nationals of that state.[40]

The creation of EU citizenship was not as smooth as the negotiators expected in 1991. The Danish constitution required a referendum on the proposed treaty which took place on 2 June 1992. The result was a very slim rejection of the treaty: 50.7% of the vote with a 83.1% turn out of eligible voters. Following substantial soul searching in Denmark, a second referendum was held on 18 May 1993 where the treaty was approved by a 56.7% in favour on a turnout of 86.5% of the voters. One of the issues which the Danish Government considered had spooked their voters in the first referendum was the creation of EU citizenship by the Treaty. To address this concern, the EU Heads of State and Government met for the first time in a procedure outside the treaties (see my criticism of this type of procedure in the first section) and in a declaration (The Edinburgh Decision, 12 December 1992) stated "...citizenship of the Union gives na-

---

37   Human Rights Act 1998; Amos, Merris. *Human Rights Law*. Bloomsbury Publishing, 2014.

38   Conservative Party, *Protecting Human Rights in the UK* available here: http://news. bbc.co.uk/2/shared/bsp/hi/pdfs/03_10_14_humanrights.pdf visited 22 August 2014.

39   C-85/96 ECR [1998] I-2691.

40   Guild, Elspeth. *The Legal Elements of European Identity: EU citizenship and migration law*. Vol. 1. Kluwer law international, 2004.

tionals of the Member States additional rights and protection as specified [in the Maastricht Treaty]. They do not in any way take the place of national citizenship."[41] The Amsterdam Treaty negotiated in 1997 added the necessary wording to the treaty provisions confirming the Edinburgh Decision.[42] It is worth noting that the Decision is clear that EU citizenship gives its holders more rights not less, than national citizenship. These new rights are on top of all the rights which people may have as a consequence of their national citizenship and does not diminish those rights in any way. Thus this first foray into EU citizenship, approved by the Danish voters, clearly was designed to clarify that the new citizenship was a source of rights. It did not and would not destroy rights which attach to national citizenship. I will examine in the next section how the draft Decision of 19 February 2016 performed exactly the opposite function – proposing to destroy EU citizenship rights.

EU citizenship began to take shape as the CJEU dealt with a steady trickle of references from national courts regarding the nature and scope of the rights. Most of these cases were about the rights of EU citizens, nationals of one Member State, on the territory of another Member State. Only rarely did they include issues of EU citizens in dispute with their state of nationality. This had already occurred in a few cases before the introduction of EU citizenship. For my purposes the most important is *Surinder Singh*[43] decided in 1992 when EU citizenship was on the table but the treaty was not yet in force. A couple, Surinder Singh (an Indian national) married Rashpal Purewal (a British citizen) in 1982 in the UK. From 1983 until 1985 Mr and Mrs Singh were employed in Germany. At the end of 1985 they returned to the UK in order to open a business. The marriage ran into difficulties and the UK authorities sought to withdraw Mr Singh's residence status thus requiring him to leave to UK or be deported. The question which came before the CJEU was what law should apply to Mr Singh's status in the UK – British law or EU law. The UK argued that as Mrs Singh was a British citizen coming back to the UK after working in another Member State she was subject on her return to British law regarding her family members. Mr Singh argued that he should be entitled to rely on EU law on family reunion even when he went to

---

41   http://www.europarl.europa.eu/summits/edinburgh/b1_en.pdf visited 23 August 2016.

42   The Article 8(1) acquired a new sentence: "Citizenship of the Union shall complement and not replace national citizenship" now Article 20 TFEU.

43   C-370/90 [1992] ECR I-4265.

the UK with his (then) wife, Mrs Singh. The CJEU held that a spouse (in the position of Mr Singh) must enjoy at least the same rights as would be granted to him or her under EU law if his or her spouse (Mrs Singh, a British citizen) entered and resided in another Member State. In other words, just as the Member States had agreed in the Edinburgh Decision, EU status (about to be incorporated into citizenship) provided additional rights to nationals of the Member States and did not detract from any existing rights under national law.

What the judgment did do was diminish the right of the UK authorities to exclude the spouses of their own nationals from living in the UK. UK family reunion policy from 1983 until 1997 applied a test to the admission of foreign spouses of British citizens whereby the couple had to prove that the primary purpose of the marriage was not to obtain access to the UK for the foreign spouse. The test was widely used to prevent husbands and fiancés from the Indian subcontinent seeking to join British national wives and would-be wives in the UK. The policy ground for the measure was to prevent marriages arranged by the families and was widely criticised by many non-governmental organisations.[44] In 1996, the year before a change of government which led to the abolition of the rule, more than 1,000 couples were barred from living together in the UK on the basis of it.[45] No such rule exists in EU family reunion law – third country national spouses of EU citizens exercising a free movement right or having exercised a free movement right are entitled to accompany or join their EU national principal on provision of evidence of the relationship (ie the marriage certificate) and proof that the EU citizen is exercising a free movement right. Thus the decision of the CJEU in *Surinder Singh* provided more rights to British citizens who exercised their free movement rights in the capacities which would be rolled into EU citizenship to live and work in another Member State and in due course to return 'home' with third country national family members than these citizens would have had under British law. The CJEU followed its reasoning in this decision in a number of later judgments including *Eind*[46] where the Dutch authorities sought to exclude the minor daughter of a Dutch na-

---

44 http://2bquk8cdew6192tsu4ilay8t.wpengine.netdna-cdn.com/wp-content/up-loads/2015/01/PrimaryPurposeRuleRuleWithNoPurpose.pdf visited 23 August 2016.

45 http://www.bbc.co.uk/news/special/politics97/news/06/0605/straw.shtml visited 23 August 2016.

46 C-291/05 [2007] ECR I-10719.

tional returning to the Netherlands after working (and enjoying family reunification with his child) in the UK. Of seminal importance are two cases from 2014 *O*[47] and *S & G*[48] where the CJEU followed its own jurisprudence in light of the citizens directive regarding the right of citizens to return 'home' with their family members or to be joined by their family members when working in one Member State but continuing to live in their home state.

I will return to this issue and what became known as the *Surinder Singh* route to family reunion in the next section. Suffice it here to note that EU citizenship was already at the end of 1992 on its way to fulfilling the promise of the Edinburgh Decision – providing EU citizens with more rights than they would have under their national law even when they were facing their Member State of underlying nationality. National authorities were prohibited from effacing rights acquired under EU law by their citizens on the return of those citizens to their home state.

On the issue of deprivation of EU citizenship, the CJEU was more reticent about interfering with national decisions. In a 2010 decision[49] Mr Rottmann, a former Austrian citizen who had naturalised as a German citizen and was resident in Germany, challenged his deprivation of German citizenship. The German authorities accused the man of fraudulent acquisition of its citizenship, a ground for withdrawal. However, Mr Rottmann by acquiring German citizenship had automatically lost his Austrian citizenship thus he was at risk of statelessness. The CJEU found that having regard to the importance which the EU treaties attach to the status of citizen of the Union, when examining a decision withdrawing naturalisation it is necessary to take into account the consequences that the decision entails for the person concerned and, if relevant, for the members of his family with regard to the loss of the rights enjoyed by every citizen of the Union. The direction of the CJEU is clear – even in the most sensitive of citizenship issues, such as deprivation, the impact of EU citizenship must be taken into account as a factor which creates rights and is loathed to permit their extinguishing.

The last decision of the CJEU which I will consider here is one which has been highly controversial with the authorities of a small number of Member States but which is particularly relevant to this discussion on

---

47   C-456/12 12 March 2014.
48   C-457/12 12 March 2014.
49   C-135/08 *Rottmann* [2010] ECR I-1449.

the rights of citizenship – *Zambrano*.[50] The issue at the heart of this decision of 2011, arriving during the period where the UK authorities were intensely whittling away at the citizenship right to enter and live in the UK, is whether EU citizens have a right to live in the EU. As in so many of these cases the facts are somewhat odd. The matter was actually referred to the CJEU by a labour tribunal in Belgium which was considering the matter whether Mr Zambrano (senior – the father of the Belgian children in question) was entitled to employment related social benefits. Mr Zambrano and his wife were Colombian nationals who had applied unsuccessfully for asylum in Belgium more than ten years before the events which came before the CJEU. In their appeal against the rejection of their asylum claims, a national court held that they could not be returned to Colombia without breaching Belgium's duty not to refoule (send back to persecution, torture or inhuman or degrading treatment) anyone. So, while the Belgian authorities refused to provide the family with any document confirming their right of residence, neither could it expel them. They resided thus for more than ten years in limbo. The couple had one child born in Colombia and two children born in Belgium. The Belgian born children were granted Belgian citizenship in order to avoid their statelessness. One of the common rules of EU citizens rights is that they attach only to those citizens who have used their right of free movement. Until the *Zambrano* judgment, it was an accepted (though as it turns out erroneous) idea that EU citizens could not use their citizenship rights in their home Member State unless they had moved and resided in another Member State. Those who never left their home Member State were classified as nationals of the relevant Member State and subject only to the law of that state (in the fields of interest to me). This is known as the wholly internal rule of EU law.

The CJEU was faced with the central issue: what is the core of EU citizenship and what is its relationship with the right to live in the EU even if the citizen has not moved and resided in another Member State?

The answer to these questions was distilled by the CJEU into one key issue: would the Belgian children be effectively required to leave the EU as a whole and live in a third country if their parents were not permitted to remain in the EU to take care of them, including by working. The court's view was that "it must be assumed that such a refusal [of residence for the parents] would lead to a situation where those children, citizens of the Union, would have to leave the territory of the Union in order to

---

50   C-34/09 *Zambrano* [2011] ECR I-1177.

accompany their parents. Similarly, if a work permit were not granted to such a person, he would risk not having sufficient resources to provide for himself and his family, which would also result in the children, citizens of the Union, having to leave the territory of the Union. In those circumstances, those citizens of the Union would, in fact, be unable to exercise the substance of the rights conferred on them by virtue of their status as citizens of the Union." (para 44). The CJEU found that citizens of the Union are entitled by their citizenship to the genuine enjoyment of the substance of the rights conferred by virtue of their status as citizens of the Union (para 45). The centre of the right of EU citizenship is the right to live in the EU. In a series of subsequent decisions resulting from a flurry of references from national courts anxious about the coherence of their national immigration rules with this core of EU citizenship, the CJEU made it clear that the right to live in the EU may mean that families have to exercise their free movement rights and go and live and work in another Member State to activate their citizenship rights.[51]

Just as the UK was moving away from the centrality of the right to live in the UK as a citizenship right, the CJEU was interpreting EU citizenship as including exactly this right as a core element. This right was being recognised even without reference to Article 3 Protocol 4 ECHR though the European Commissioner for Human Rights was exploring both the extent of the right to leave one's country as a corollary of the right to live in one's country.[52] Obviously a clash was in the offing.

British Citizenship without Rights or EU Citizenship: The UK Supreme Court Decides

In March 2015 the UK Supreme Court handed down judgment in the case of *Pham*.[53] The matter revealed, once again, rather odd facts. Mr Pham was born a Vietnamese national in 1983. In 1989 he and his family sought asylum in the UK (after a period in Hong Kong) and in 1995 they were granted British citizenship. By 2011, the British security services had come

---

51   C-256/11 *Dereci* [2011] ECR I-1135; C-86/12 *Alokpa* 10 October 2013 among others.

52   Commissioner for Human Rights *The Right to Leave a country* Issue Paper, Council of Europe 2013 available here: http://www.coe.int/t/commissioner/source/prems/prems150813_GBR_1700_TheRightToLeaveACountry_web.pdf visited 23 August 2016.

53   *Pham v Secretary of State for the Home Department* [2015] UKSC 19.

to the conclusion that Mr Pham posed a threat to the safety and security of the UK on account of his Islamist beliefs and actions, according to the services, including receiving terrorist training from Al Qaida members in Yemen.[54] The US authorities sought his extradition to that country to stand trial (details of the charges are not included in the Supreme Court judgment). He was extradited in February 2015, tried in New York for his efforts in support of al Qaeda in the Arabian Peninsula ("AQAP"), a designated foreign terrorist organization and sentenced to 40 years imprisonment there.[55]

On 22 December 2011 the UK Secretary of State notified Mr Pham that she was depriving him of his British citizenship as this would be conducive to the (British) public good. She determined that he would not be stateless as he retained his Vietnamese citizenship. Mr Pham challenged this deprivation. The issue which came before the Supreme Court was whether or not Mr Pham would in fact be stateless if the Secretary of State had her way regarding his deprivation of British citizenship. Here the facts become quite astonishing. Mr Pham produced evidence from the Vietnamese authorities that they did not consider that he was a Vietnamese citizen. The UK Supreme Court, working from English translations of Vietnamese legislation, came to the conclusion that the Vietnamese authorities were wrong about their own law. As one of the their Lordships (Lord Mance) put it "All that happened is that the Vietnamese Government has, when subsequently informed by the British Government of its intention to deport the appellant, declined to accept that he was or is a Vietnamese national." (para 66). The implication is of bad faith on the part of the Vietnamese authorities and/or their incompetence in the interpretation of Vietnamese law (which the UK Supreme Court could do so much better working from translations and without the impediment of training in Vietnamese jurisprudence).

Mr Pham argued that his deprivation of British citizenship would deprive him also of EU citizenship. This claim occupied all of their Lordships to a substantial extent though they were all agreed that there was no need to refer any preliminary questions to the CJEU. This matter would be determined in accordance with British judicial sovereignty even though what was at stake was the meaning of EU citizenship. While

---

54   These allegations by the UK security services were never the subject of judicial scrutiny according to the Supreme Court.

55   https://www.justice.gov/usao-sdny/pr/member-al-qaeda-arabian-peninsula-sentenced-40-years-prison-manhattan-federal-court visited 23 August 2016.

most of the seven judge bench were happy to agree with the lead opinion of Lord Carnwath on the Vietnamese citizenship issue and only added a few extra words, three of them (Mance, Sumption and Reed) had much to add on the issue of EU citizenship – all of them in agreement that they were competent to determine the issue because the interpretation of British citizenship was their job. There is (once again) a deep anxiety among the judges regarding the possible application of EU citizenship rights to do what the Edinburgh Decision promised – add rights in addition to national citizenship not limit those rights.

All of the judges in the Supreme Court who expressed a view on why EU citizenship rights could not add rights which British citizenship denied focused on the issue of proportionality. The problem to be resolved was whether the EU principle of proportionality would hinder the British Secretary of State in her decision to deprive Mr Pham of British citizenship. The judges expressed a range of views about proportionality and what it means and how it might fit into British law but the clearest view was that of Lord Mance in an opinion largely concurring with Lord Carnwath (and with whom three of the other judges agreed). In order to deal with the proportionality issue in EU law which was clearly worrying all the judges, he chose to undermine the principle altogether. "In short, proportionality is – as Professor Dr Lübbe-Wolff (former judge of the Bundesverfassungsgericht which originated the term's modern use) put it in The Principle of Proportionality in the case-law of the German Federal Constitutional Court (2014) 34 HRLJ 12, 16-17 – "a tool directing attention to different aspects of what is implied in any rational assessment of the reasonableness of a restriction", "just a rationalising heuristic tool"." (para 96). One can sense the relief in the court – proportionality is just a rationalising heuristic tool (assuming that everyone agreed on what a rationalising heuristic tool might be).

In any event, a simple rationalising heuristic tool was not going to be allowed to get in the way of the discretion of the Secretary of State as informed by the intelligence services about what is conducive to the public good in the UK. And no EU tool was going to be allowed to apportion to Mr Pham citizenship rights which exceeding those which the Secretary of State was willing to accord him. When Mr Pham gets out of prison in the USA many years hence, it is unlikely that he will be able to return to the UK as a citizen although he is married to a British national and has British children with her. Whether the US authorities will be able to expel Mr Pham to the Vietnam will be a matter for them.

Conclusions

In this section I have examined two citizenships – British and EU - from the perspective of the rights which they confer on their holders. While British citizenship confers fewer and fewer rights on its holders, not only in terms of durability but also in terms of entitlement to enter and reside on the territory, EU citizenship has taken a different turn, increasing the rights of EU citizens to reside in the EU and to enjoy rights which their home authorities are unwilling to accord to them (such as family reunion, to which I will return in the next section). The essence of the concept of citizenship is at stake in this divergence. What does it mean to be a citizen and what are the limits of state powers to diminish, remove and extinguish citizenship. The answers to both these questions are entirely different when one compares the UK and the EU. On the one hand, the UK has moved away from the recognition and delivery of citizenship rights to its people. Particularly after 2002, a series of laws have diminished the certainty of British citizens as to the durability of their citizenship or any rights at all which might be attached to it. On the other hand, the interpretation of EU citizenship by the CJEU has moved in the opposite direction. This new citizenship only created in 1993 has gained flesh and power through the decisions of the CJEU. The court has even been willing to take on one of the sacred cows of the EU, the wholly internal rule, to find that EU citizens must always be entitled to live in the EU.

Citizens and Their Monstrous Families

There is a beauty and the beast story that I'd like to tell you, because like many fairytales, it shows that things are never quite as they seem and that surprises can spring from any quarter. "The Wedding of Sir Gawain and Dame Ragnell" is a verse romance written in the mid-fifteenth century by a forgotten and nameless English poet. It reworks the familiar fairytale theme of a young man's union with a she-monster, and by the way produces a happy story, at first bawdy, later tender, about the possibility of mutual love and trust, against the odds.

> MARINA WARNER *Managing Monsters: Six Myths of Our Time –*
> *The Reith Lectures 1994*

Introduction

Just as the idea of citizenship is dear to people, so too the idea of family is a cherished concept. The family and in particular the family which has been recognised by the state (marriage or civil partnership) enjoys protections far beyond other forms of union no matter how durable which have not been notified and accepted by state authorities.[1] The state's role in recognising marriage and civil partnerships as worthy of extra protection also forms the basis of rules around what types of marriage or civil partnership will be acknowledged. The struggle of same sex partners for recognition and state protection of their relationships is a story of the final quarter of the 20th century and the first of the 21st century.[2] Only in 2013 did the UK pass an act allowing same sex partners to marry.[3] Same sex marriage has moved in most of Europe and the USA from being a

---

1   http://researchbriefings.parliament.uk/ResearchBriefing/Summary/SN03372 #fullreport visited 24 August 2016.

2   Wintemute, Robert, and Mads Tønnesson Andenæs, eds. *Legal recognition of same-sex partnerships: A study of national, European and international law.* Hart Publishing, 2001.

3   http://www.legislation.gov.uk/ukpga/2013/30/enacted visited 24 August 2016.

monstrous idea to a signalling issue on the basis of which is determined who are the monsters, now they are the opponents of same sex marriage.[4]

While the gender of parties to a marriage has become increasingly unimportant in the UK and EU, their citizenship and immigration status has become ever more important. The idea that foreigners are seeking to avoid deportation or removal from the UK by getting married and so ever more coercive action needs to be taken by the authorities to prevent such abuse has moved into mainstream logic.[5] The history of immigration controls on family members has been well documented not least by Helena Wray[6] the title of whose book – a stranger in the home – is most revealing about UK authorities fears about foreign spouses (and other family members). The underlying fear includes though is not limited to the fear of contamination.[7] In order to off set this risk, state authorities seek ever more draconian ways of limiting foreign spouses arrival in the UK – for the moment the most popular is a mandatory high income threshold of £18,600 before family reunion will be allowed. The level of income support (social benefits) for a couple over 18 years of age is £5,972.20. So a couple where one member is a foreign national has to have an income of over three times what the state considers appropriate to provide to an indigent but indigenous couple. Of course, a couple where one member is a foreigner is prohibited from claiming this support (or most other types of social benefits) which are classified as public funds to which foreigners are prohibited access without endangering their immigration status (until their acquire indefinite leave to remain or in a few other exceptional categories). One non-governmental organisation calculated that 47% of the UK working population does not make enough money to enjoy family reunion with a foreign spouse.[8] At the time of writing a legal challenge to the income threshold was pending before the UK Supreme Court which

---

4   http://www.pinknews.co.uk/2015/07/07/ryan-reynolds-i-support-same-sex-mar-
        riage-because-im-not-a-monster/ visited 24 August 2016.

5   http://www.bbc.com/news/uk-scotland-south-scotland-21441822 visited 24 August
        2016.

6   Wray, Helena. *Regulating marriage migration into the UK: A stranger in the home.*
        Ashgate Publishing, Ltd., 2011.

7   https://www.theguardian.com/commentisfree/2013/dec/15/uk-immigration-poli-
        cy-britons-spouses-trauma visited 24 August 2016.

8   http://www.migrantsrights.org.uk/blog/2014/06/18600-income-requirement-pric-
        ing-uk-workers-out-family-life visited 24 August 2016.

heard the case in February 2016 but has not yet decided it.[9] The foreign spouse must also pass an English language test (with some exceptions).

As Wray has shown, the rules of family reunion for British citizens with foreign family members have made steady progress from restrictive to more restrictive and onwards. Rare reversals by a Government, such as the abolition of the primary purpose rule (discussed in the previous section), are very few and far between. Similarly, reversals by the courts are rare. One outstanding example from 2008 was the UK Supreme Court's decision that the requirement for couples where at least one party is a foreigner to obtain a certificate of approval from the authorities before marrying (except where the marriage would take place in a Church of England ceremony) was inconsistent with the right to marry in the ECHR.[10] This decision was supported by the ECtHR which concurred with the Supreme Court.[11]

It would seem that there are a number of reasons why foreign family members are monstrous to the UK authorities. The first seems to be because they are foreign and therefore are likely to want to cheat the (ever more coercive) immigration system. Secondly, they are dangerous as they and their spouses might be poor and seek social benefits (so these have to be forbidden to them). They might work thus taking a job from a British citizen, according to the zero sum game fallacy about the labour market to which successive British Governments pander, notwithstanding evidence from a Home Office report of 2014 which, after a detailed examination of the available sources of information found that there is no statistically significant displacement of "UK natives".[12] But natives and monsters still get together and monstrous families have been a theme of British immigration law for more than 30 years. When the "UK natives" instead of becoming more native, start marrying she and he-monsters their offspring risk becoming less "native".[13] Lurking behind the facts of

---

9   *R (on the application of MM (Lebanon)) (AP) (Appellant) v Secretary of State for the Home Department (Respondent)*Case ID UKSC 2015/0011.

10   *R. (on the application of Baiai and others) v Secretary of State for the Home Department* [2008] UKHL 53.

11   *O'Donoghue v UK* Application no. 34848/07, 14 December 2010.

12   https://www.gov.uk/government/uploads/system/uploads/attachment_data/file/287287/occ109.pdf visited 24 August 2016.

13   Groenendijk, Kees. "Family reunification as a right under Community law." *European Journal of Migration and Law* 8.2 (2006): 215. In this seminal article, Groenendijk sets out the evidence that Dutch (and British) family reunion rules become more and more restrictive as citizens who used to be immigrants but are now citizens

many of the family reunion cases which have come before the CJEU is the fact that the citizen seeking family reunion has, as the Germans so delicately put it, an immigration background.[14] In the other cases, it is the unwelcome marriage choices of "natives" with foreigners.[15]

EU family reunion rules for EU citizens have barely changed since the first regulation was adopted in 1961.[16] The principle is and remains the entitlement of family members (of any nationality) to accompany or join their EU citizen principal to a host Member State and to enjoy the same rights as the principal there. The position of the family members is assimilated to that of the principal. The group of family members with this right are spouses (and registered partners on the basis of equal treatment with nationals of the host state if such partnerships are recognised), children under 21 or over 21 if dependent on the EU citizen and his or her spouse, family members in the ascending and descending lines if dependent on the EU citizen and his or her spouse. Very few conditions can be placed on family reunion. EU citizens who are workers or self employed cannot be required to prove evidence that they can support themselves or their family members without recourse to public funds. No comprehensive sickness insurance requirement applies to them. For students,[17] pensioners and the economically inactive an income threshold can be applied but it cannot exceed the threshold at which nationals of the state become eligible for social assistance. There are many nuances in the rules and provisions for wider family members to join the EU citizen principal but for my purposes this family of multigenerational close relationships is sufficient.

The EU rules offend against UK national rules in many ways. First, the lack or limitation of the income threshold, secondly the lack of a minimum age for spouses before family reunion, thirdly, family reunion rights for all children up to the age of 21 and rights for the over 21s who are dependent, fourthly, the right to family reunion with dependent parents

---

and their children began to claim the right to family life with their family members in the countries of origin of their parents or grandparents.

14   See for instance, http://www.migrationpolicy.org/research/coordinating-immigrant-integration-germany-mainstreaming-federal-and-local-levels visited 25 August 2016.

15   Guild, Elspeth. "Free Movement of EU Citizens and their Family Members" New Journal of European Criminal Law 2(2016): 34.

16   Regulation 15/61 OJ No 57, 26.8.1961, p. 1073/61.

17   Exceptionally, students do not enjoy a family reunion right with relatives in the direct ascending line.

and grandparents, fifthly, no housing requirement, sixthly, no prohibition on access to public funds for workers the self employed and their families, seventh, no duty to get prior approval from state authorities to marry, eighth, no interrogation into the reasons for the marriage (but with a prohibition on sham marriages only), ninth, no high fees – at the time of writing a visa for a spouse costs €1,458 or GBP 1195. Most offensive of all, family reunion is a right for EU citizens, not a privilege to be granted or withheld at the discretion of the state.

Monstrous Families in the BREXIT Negotiations

In the first section I examined the negotiations between the EU institutions and the UK before the UK referendum on remaining or leaving the EU. I indicated there that I would return to the content of the draft Decision of 19 February 2016 where the parties in a most *sui generis* manner undertook to pass a Decision on condition that the UK voted to remain in the EU. In this section I will now deliver on that undertaking to examine the content of the draft Decision regarding families.

In the letter of (then) Prime Minister Cameron to the President of the EU Council of 10 November 2015,[18] he set out the UK Government's concerns about EU citizens and their family reunion rights as follows: "We need to crack down on the abuse of free movement, an issue on which I have found wide support in my discussions with colleagues. This includes tougher and longer re-entry bans for fraudsters and people who collude in sham marriages. It means addressing the fact that it is easier for an EU citizen to bring a non-EU spouse to Britain than it is for a British citizen to do the same." What the UK Government demanded from the EU was that it adjust its too generous family reunion laws to comply with British national law. The possibility that a more reasonable solution might be to change British national family reunion rules so that British citizens at home could enjoy the same rights as their EU citizen neighbours is not an option contemplated by the Prime Minister. Because EU family reunion rules are more generous that British ones those benefiting from them are suspect. Fraudsters and sham marriages are hiding behind non-British EU citizens' exercise of their right to family reunion.

---

18   https://www.gov.uk/government/uploads/system/uploads/attachment_data/file/475679/Donald_Tusk_letter.pdf visited 25 August 2016.

The notification of the President of the EU Council to the Member States on the state of the negotiations dated 2 February 2016[19] makes no specific reference to the issue of family reunion. Instead President Tusk refers to a draft Commission Declaration "on a number of issues relating to better fighting abuse of free movement." But the notification insists that "we must fully respect the current treaties, in particular the principles of freedom of movement and non-discrimination." The draft Declaration of the European Commission,[20] however, deals quite precisely with the issue.

The Commission states in its draft that, on the conditions being fulfilled (a positive referendum result in the UK) it will adopt a proposal to complement the citizens directive (where the family reunion rights are to be found) in order to exclude from the scope of free movement rights third country nationals who had no prior lawful residence in a Member State before marrying an Union citizen or who marry a Union citizen only after the Union citizen has established residence in the host Member State. The Commission states that in such cases the host Member State's immigration law will apply to the third country national family member.

This undertaking by the Commission is rife with problems. The two conditions proposed, have already been the subject of litigation before the CJEU which has held them inconsistent with the right of free movement of persons and indeed contrary to the internal market. The first condition – that a third country national without lawful residence in a Member State who marries an EU citizen is excluded from the scope of free movement rights – contradicts the constant jurisprudence of the CJEU. In *MRAX*[21] decided in 2002, the court was faced with the same question – can a third country national who is irregularly present (in the judgment the CJEU delicately refers to third country nationals whose visas have expired but it amounts to the same thing as the reasoning of the judgment also expressly includes those third country nationals who may have entered the state irregularly as well). It held that "a Member State may neither refuse to issue a residence permit to a third country national who is married to a national of a Member State and entered the territory of that Member State lawfully, nor issue an order expelling him from the

---

19   http://www.consilium.europa.eu/en/press/press-releases/2016/02/02-letter-tusk-
       proposal-new-settlement-uk/ visited 25 August 2016.
20   Council Document EUCO 8/16.
21   C-459/99 [2002] ECR I-5691.

territory, on the sole ground that his visa expired before he applied for a residence permit." (para 91). The legislation under consideration was the directive which preceded the citizens directive adopted in 2004 but covers the same territory. The CJEU was also required subsequently to clarify that the citizens directive increases the rights of EU citizens and does not diminish them in relation to the previous legislation.[22]

This fairly clear judgment did not stop some Member States from continuing to argue that they were entitled to require third country national family members of EU citizens exercising rights to have nationally issued entry or residence permits. The UK got a 'win' on this matter in 2003 when the CJEU, as it regretted in a subsequent judgment,[23] reversed itself and found that a third country national spouse of an EU citizen had to passed through the eye of the needle of national law in some Member State before he or she could come within the personal scope of EU free movement rights in line with his or her EU citizen principal.[24] The CJEU reversed itself on this matter and reverted to the *MRAX* position in 2005 in the context of a Commission infringement procedure against Spain for requiring third country national spouses of EU citizens exercising treaty free movement rights in Spain to have a residence visa issued in accordance with national law before being entitled to EU family reunion rights.[25] Yet a number of Member States were still not satisfied that EU

---

22   C-127/08 *Metock* [2008] ECR I-6241 "As is apparent from recital 3 in the preamble to Directive 2004/38, it aims in particular to 'strengthen the right of free movement and residence of all Union citizens', so that Union citizens cannot derive less rights from that directive than from the instruments of secondary legislation which it amends or repeals." (para 59).

23   C-127/08 *Metock* [2008] ECR I-6241 "It is true that the Court held in paragraphs 50 and 51 of *Akrich* that, in order to benefit from the rights provided for in Article 10 of Regulation No 1612/68, the national of a non-member country who is the spouse of a Union citizen must be lawfully resident in a Member State when he moves to another Member State to which the citizen of the Union is migrating or has migrated. However, that conclusion must be reconsidered. The benefit of such rights cannot depend on the prior lawful residence of such a spouse in another Member State (see, to that effect, *MRAX*, paragraph 59, and Case C-157/03 *Commission* v *Spain*, paragraph 28)." (para 58).

24   C-109/01 *Akrich* [2003] ECR I-9607 paras 50 and 51.

25   C-157/03 *Commission v Spain* [2005] ECR I-2911 "Consequently, the residence visa requirement laid down by the Spanish rules in order to obtain a residence permit and, consequently, the refusal to issue such a permit to a third-country national who is a member of the family of a Community national, on the ground that he or she should first have applied for a residence visa at the Spanish consulate in their

law really required them to acknowledge the right of EU citizens exercising treaty rights to enjoy family reunion with third country national spouses irrespective of the status which national law might have allocated to the spouse.

The CJEU was required to clarify once again this right in *Metock*[26] when, as mentioned above, it expressly disallowed its decision in *Akrich*. The CJEU explained that "[T]he refusal of the host Member State to grant rights of entry and residence to the family members of a Union citizen is such as to discourage that citizen from moving to or residing in that Member State, even if his family members are not already lawfully resident in the territory of another Member State." (para 64). Further it reasoned that to allow the Member States exclusive competence to grant or refuse entry into and residence in their territory to third country national family members of Union citizens who have not already resided lawfully in another Member State would have the effect that the freedom of movement of Union citizens in a host Member State would vary from one Member State to another, according to the provisions of national law concerning immigration, with some Member States permitting entry and residence of family members of a Union citizen and other Member States refusing them (para 67). The CJEU made it clear that this right was not simply a result of secondary legislation but an integral part of the internal market.[27]

The evolution of this jurisprudence and its analysis is not new. Many outstanding EU scholars have discussed it and set out clearly its scope and limits.[28] There is nothing new in what I have set out here except for

---

last place of domicile thus constitutes a measure contrary to the provisions of Directives 68/360, 73/148 and 90/365." (para 28).

26   C-127/08 *Metock* ECR [2008] I-6241.

27   C-127/08 *Metock* ECR [2008] I-6241 "That would not be compatible with the objective set out in Article 3(1)(c) EC of an internal market characterised by the abolition, as between Member States, of obstacles to the free movement of persons. Establishing an internal market implies that the conditions of entry and residence of a Union citizen in a Member State whose nationality he does not possess are the same in all the Member States. Freedom of movement for Union citizens must therefore be interpreted as the right to leave any Member State, in particular the Member State whose nationality the Union citizen possesses, in order to become established under the same conditions in any Member State other than the Member State whose nationality the Union citizen possesses." (para 68).

28   See for instance Costello, Cathryn. "Metock: free movement and "normal family life" in the Union." *Common Market law review* 46.2 (2009): 587-622; Martin,

the astonishing undertaking of the Commission to reverse the constant and much litigated jurisprudence of the CJEU by means of a proposal, not even an amendment to secondary legislation, to make a change which the CJEU has held would be contrary to the Treaties and the internal market.

The second undertaking of the Commission in its attack on family reunion rights of EU citizens contained in the draft Declaration of 2 February attached to President Tusk's letter was to exclude from the personal scope of EU free movement of persons, once again in the form of a proposal which would not even constitute an amendment to secondary legislation, any third country national who marries an EU citizen after he or she has established him or herself in the host Member State. The same fundamental flaws apply to this undertaking on the basis of the same jurisprudence as I have outlined above. I shall not repeat all the arguments again. What I find so disappointing in this Declaration of the Commission is the profound betrayal of EU citizens, the treaties, the CJEU and rule of law in the EU. From the institution charged with upholding the treaties impartially this is really unacceptable. The Commission itself has here associated itself with the ideology of the monstrous family as one where third country national spouses contaminate EU citizens and the EU itself. In the reasoning of the Commission this monstrous family needs to be subject to special obstacles and prohibitions on family life.

The Commission adds two more declarations to allow Member States to fight against the monstrous family. First, it undertakes to permit Member States to address specific cases of abuse of free movement rights by EU citizens returning to their home Member State (of nationality) with their third country national family members "where residence in the host Member State has not been sufficiently genuine to create or strengthen family life and had the purpose of evading the application of national immigration rules." This promise once again offends against the jurisprudence of the CJEU. In a decision of 2014[29] it held that where, during the genuine residence of the Union citizen in the host Member State under EU law, family life is created or strengthened in that Member State, the effectiveness of the treaty rights of Union citizens as such require that the citizen's family life in the host Member State may continue on returning

---

D. "Comments on Forster (Case C-158/07 of 18 November 2008), Metock (Case C-127/08 of 25 July 2008) and Huber (Case C-524/06 of 16 December 2008)." *Eur. J. Migration & L.* 11 (2009): 95.

29   C-456/12 *O* 12 March 2014.

to his or her home Member State. This takes the form of a derived right of residence for the third-country national family member. The court reasoned that if no such derived right of residence were granted, the Union citizen could be discouraged from leaving his or her home Member State in order to exercise his or her EU citizenship right of residence. The EU citizen would be uncertain whether he or she will be able to continue in the home Member State a family life with his immediate family members which has been created or strengthened in the host Member State (para 54).

The (British) Advocate-General in the case had proposed to the court that it find that the right of EU citizens to return home with their third country national family members should be made dependent on proof that the EU citizen had integrated in the host Member State by creating sufficiently genuine links there so that the residence was more than merely a mechanism to avoid stricter national family reunion rules. The CJEU expressly declined to follow the Advocate-General in this line of reasoning. It tied the interpretation of genuine residence exclusively to residence as defined in the citizens directive with no additional requirements.

Stepping back for just a moment from the monstrousness of the Commission's disregard for the authority of the CJEU, what was the Commission offering the UK by this undertaking? Effectively it was promising that the UK could prevent British citizens who go to live in other Member States in exercise of EU citizenship rights and who are joined by third country national family members in the host state from returning to the UK with those family members. So while the British citizen could always go back to the UK, their third country national family members who were living with them in the host Member State could be excluded. In such circumstances, they would be stranded in the host Member State unable to join their EU citizen principal in the UK. Who were the families which the British Government wanted to exclude from the UK? Clearly this promise of the Commission is about British citizens, not nationals of other EU Member States. The objective of this promise to the UK is to enable the UK to exclude its own disobedient citizens who have insisted on marrying third country nationals against the wishes of the British Government. Instead, these families would become the 'problem' of contamination of another Member State. In effect the British citizen would not be able to go back to his or her country of nationality without abandoning his or her family members in the host Member State. This is a horrible dilemma to place a citizen in. It is also fairly monstrous behaviour towards the other

27 Member States – the Commission is promising the UK that it can effectively prevent families of British citizens from coming back to the UK and thus requiring one of the other 27 Member State to continue to host them on its territory. If these families are so monstrous for the UK why would they not be monstrous also for the host Member State? The logic is one of Commission favoritism to the UK.

Finally, the Commission undertakes in its declaration that it will clarify the concept of a marriage of convenience (which it helpfully indicates is not protected by Union law) to cover also a marriage which is maintained for the purpose of enjoying a right of residence by a third country national family member. The issue of marriages of convenience had already been the subject of substantial discussion among the Member States and the Commission. The Commission issued, in 2014, a 50 page document for the Member States entitled *Helping national authorities fight abuses of the right to free movement: Handbook on addressing the issue of alleged marriages of convenience between EU citizens and non-EU nationals in the context of EU law on free movement of EU citizens.*[30] This lengthy document goes into tremendous detail trying to pin down exactly what a marriage of convenience is and how to identify such an abuse without interfering with the right of free movement of EU citizens.

The promise in the declaration which the Commission makes to take even more action to help Member States attack marriages which they designate as of convenience[31] goes much further than the handbook. Here the Commission proposes rules for attacking marriages which are maintained (not entered into) for the purpose of enjoying a right of residence. So these marriages, which the Commission suggests will be classified as marriages of convenience are not those which were entered into for the purpose of convenience. These marriages as the Commission's own handbook sets out need to be identified from the outset. The marriages which the Commission now intends to allow Member States to attack are those which were not marriages of convenience at the outset (raising the question whether there are marriages which are neither genuine nor marriages of convenience but something in a grey area between the two – rather dangerous legal territory one would suggest) but become

---

30   26 September 2014 SWD (2014) 284 final.

31   For an interesting empirical examination of this issue see Infantino, Federica. "Bordering 'fake' marriages? The everyday practices of control at the consulates of Belgium, France and Italy in Casablanca." *Etnografia e ricerca qualitativa* 7.1 (2014): 27-48.

marriages of convenience with the passage of time. Just how a marriage becomes a marriage of convenience over time is a matter of speculation, all of which goes in the direction of unacceptable interferences with the private and family life of EU citizens.

As in respect of the other undertakings of the Commission, this one too, offends against the very long standing jurisprudence of the CJEU. In 1984 the court first found that a marriage which had not been dissolved but where the parties no longer lived together was still a marriage in EU law. The CJEU was unconvinced by arguments that a marriage could, with the passage of time, become no longer valid for immigration purposes merely because the parties had tired of one another or chose to live separately. The CJEU held that if one of the parties is a third country national he or she remains protected by EU family reunion law and cannot be made subject to national immigration law because the marriage has encountered difficulties. Only divorce can end a marriage.[32] This jurisprudence was confirmed by the court in 2014.[33]

On 19 February 2016 the Council Conclusions were published with the final version of the Draft Decision and associated documents (including the Commission's Declarations). Section D(c) on social benefits and free movement states that those enjoying the right to free movement must abide by the laws of the host Member State. Here, the Heads of State and Government addressed the issue of third country national family members. It confirmed that Member States are able to take action to prevent abuse of rights, including to address cases of contracting or maintaining marriages of convenience of third country nationals for the purpose of making use of free movement as a route for regularising unlawful stay in a Member State. Further the Heads of State and Government stated that Member States may address the case of making use of free movement as a route for bypassing national immigration rules applying to third country nationals. Thus the Heads of State and Government themselves decided not to pay too much attention to the binding nature of the decisions of the CJEU. The Commission's declaration attached to the draft Decision remains unchanged from the draft of 2 February, with all the flaws outlined in this section.

---

32   267/83 *Diatta* [1984] ECR 567.

33   C-244/13 *Ogieriakhi* 10 July 2014.

Conclusions

Article 16(3) of the Universal Declaration of Human Rights 1948 states that the family is the natural and fundamental group unit of society and is entitled to protection by society and the State. All EU Member States subscribe to the Universal Declaration and are committed to its principles. In stark contrast to the importance which the Universal Declaration ascribes to the family as the fundamental group unit of society, when the family consists of citizens and third country nationals its entitlement to protection by the State seems to evaporate at least in some European countries. In the case of the UK and the BREXIT negotiations, the undesirability of third country national family members, particularly in the form of foreign spouses is made explicit. These families will not be entitled to protection but will be subject to obstacles and hurdles to their family life which are very different from the treatment accorded to spouses who have the 'right' citizenships. In the BREXIT documents, the UK pushed the other Member States and the EU institutions to accept that third country national spouses are a risk of such proportion that draconian measures are justified to examine and prevent their exercise of family life with British citizens (and by extension all EU citizens). There may well have been some other Member States which were quietly pleased to have possible new powers, too, to attack marriages where one spouse is a foreign national. Behind this discourse of risk, fraud, threat of third country national spouses what is going on? Clearly, these people are not only unwanted but risky for the state. Citizens who insist on marrying foreigners are themselves risks and deserve to be prevent from enjoying family reunion. These are thus monstrous families which contaminate the state and must be excluded.

That the Member States and the EU institutions should have permitted themselves to be pushed into participating in such a grotesque spectacle is shameful for everyone involved.

Monstrous Fears

Reason can be awake and beget monsters.
Extreme, fantastical, and insubstantial as they are,
they materialise real desires, fears, they embody meaning
at a deep, psychic level. We're living in a new age
of faith of sorts, of myth-making, of monsters, of chimeras.
And these chimeras define identity – especially the role of men.

MARINA WARNER *Managing Monsters: Six Myths of Our Times – The Reith*
Lectures 1994

Introduction

Michael Gove, the former British Justice Minister and one of the leaders of the Leave campaign, was quoted in a newspaper friendly to his views that "Revealing new research from Vote Leave, the official lead Brexit campaign, Mr Gove said anywhere between 2.6 million and five million extra EU migrants could come to Britain by 2030. Mr Gove said 88 million extra people would be granted the right to live and work in Britain due to the EU's commitment to Albania, Macedonia, Montenegro, Serbia and Turkey all joining the Brussels-based bloc."[1]

My purpose here is not to enter into a debate with the Leave campaign on their claims about the rights of EU citizens from present and possibly future Member States to come to live and work in the UK. This has been very effectively examined elsewhere during the campaign.[2] Instead it is the transformation of the right of free movement from something normal to a fearful and monstrous act (always by others) which is my concern here. The comparison I would like to make is between two types of statement. The first appears ridiculous to any British citizen: "64.1 million people living in the UK are entitled to move even tomorrow if they wish, to Oxford, a town of 150,000. This would swamp the town creating

---

1   http://www.express.co.uk/news/politics/672233/EU-referendum-Michael-Gove-Vote-Leave-UK-population-five-million-Brexit-EU-migration 20 May 2016, visited 29 August 2016.

2   See for instance BBC Radio 4's authoritative statistical programme, More or Less, series on the referendum by numbers which was run in five parts ending on 18 June 2016: http://www.bbc.co.uk/programmes/b006qshd/episodes/player .

massive housing, schooling and health service shortages." This statement appears immediately odd and out of kilter. Yes, the population of the UK has the right to move to Oxford if it so wishes but no one expects that to happen or thinks that measures need to be taken to stop them doing so. The other statement is that of former Justice Minister Gove: the 88 million inhabitants of Albania, Macedonia, Montenegro, Serbia and Turkey will in the future all be entitled to move to the UK to take jobs. This statement does not seem so monstrous, instead it appears to demand a reasoned response. Someone is expected to explain how what has now been transformed into a threat (free movement of persons) can be controlled and prevented. Between the two statements a profound shift of logic has occurred. The possibility of the whole of the UK moving to Oxford is obviously silly and the reader is immediately encouraged to think of the practical problems – housing, jobs etc. The people who might be moving to Oxford are equivalent to us the readers and we do not expect our behaviour to be bizarre. Yet, the possibility of the whole populations of five countries moving to the UK does not share the same logic. The fear at work is that those people are different from us, they may behave in bizarre ways. The further fear which is generated is that because they are different (of implicit poverty) moving to the UK might be a reasonable option for them (but not for us).

The core difference between the two statements is that the first rests on an accepted idea that citizens are entitled to move freely within their state. The second rests on the idea that EU citizens (and future citizens) are not and will never be real citizens. The threat being expressed is that free movement of people within the territory of the EU (the 28 current Member States and future Member States) is a monstrous right which must be curtailed before havoc occurs. Fear can be engendered more easily in the second instance than in the first without destablising what can be sensitive internal divisions within states. The fears which are conjured up may be extreme, fantastical and insubstantial but that does not destroy their power to re-order identity. The mechanism which I want to examine here is the move from EU citizen to immigrant which takes place after 2013 and in which the UK is a key player. The end place is the acceptance by the Member States and the EU institutions that the UK should be entitled to an emergence break on free movement of workers in the BREXIT negotiations.

Setting the Stage

In April 2013, the interior ministries of four Member States, Austria, Germany, the Netherlands and the UK,[3] wrote to the then Presidency of the EU Council (Ireland) expressing their concern that "currently, a number of municipalities, towns and cities in various Member States are under considerable strain by certain immigrants from other Member States".[4] This letter was written in the context of the end of transitional restrictions on free movement of workers from Bulgaria and Romania which would come to a final end on 1 January 2014. Transitional restrictions on EU 8 workers had been lifted for all Member States on 30 April 2011. While the UK had not applied transitional restrictions on EU 8 workers (though it put in place a mandatory worker registration scheme) it had in place restrictions on Bulgarian and Romanian workers. The four interior ministries which signed the letter represented some of the Member States where a debate about access to social benefits for nationals of the EU 8 in particular was politically volatile among parties on the right.[5]

The letter is worth examining in some detail as it contains the first serious attack on EU citizenship by four important Member States (or their interior ministries at least) since the citizenship's creation in 1993. First, the interior ministers confirm in the second paragraph that they are fully committed to the common European right to freedom of movement. They reassure the Presidency that they will always "welcome Union citizens who move to another EU country to work or to take up professional training or university studies." Already here quite a lot of EU citizens have been excluded such as those who are job seekers, self employed, pensioners and the economically inactive (but self sufficient). Further, as the interior ministers make clear, EU citizens are not real 'citizens' in the same way as people are citizens of their country. The interior ministers make it clear that EU citizens are only entitled to the central citizenship right to live on the territory of the entity of citizenship where they fulfil specific conditions. Relying on the wording of Article 21 TFEU, the four

---

3   The Home Secretary who signed the letter for the UK was Theresa May, who became Prime Minister after the BREXIT referendum outcome.

4   http://docs.dpaq.de/3604-130415_letter_to_presidency_final_1_2.pdf visited 29 August 2016.

5   This report produced for the European Parliament is particularly succinct about the subject: http://www.europarl.europa.eu/RegData/bibliotheque/briefing/2014/140808/LDM_BRI(2014)140808_REV1_EN.pdf visited 29 August 2016.

ministers insist that EU citizens may only move and reside subject to the
limitations and conditions laid down in the treaties and by the measures
adopted to give them effect (in particular the citizens directive).

By the fourth paragraph of the letter, however, the four interior ministers no longer refer to EU citizens, instead people exercising the EU free
movement rights have become 'immigrants'. The word is clearly pejora-
tive – it is evident that in speaking of 'immigrants' the interior ministers
are referring to people who are of dubious character, not wanted where
they are and a burden on the host State. They do not mince their words
in this regard – these immigrants are causing considerable strain on the
ministers' municipalities, towns and cities. Further, instead of exercising
their rights as citizens, according to the ministers they are availing themselves of the opportunities that freedom of movement provides. The language is that of 'free riders' – people who snatch up opportunities created
by legal regimes when they are not the 'intended' beneficiaries. According to the ministers these people are not proper beneficiaries because
they do not fulfil the requirements for the exercise of the free movement
right.

The problem which these 'free-riding' immigrants cause is clearly
identified by the ministers. They create burdens for the host societies
with considerable additional costs. These costs are clustered, according
to the ministers, in the provision of schooling, health care and adequate
accommodation. The ministers distinguish three types of commitment:
first, their obligation to protect the rights of those Union citizens who
exercise their right to freedom of movement in accordance with EU
secondary law. Secondly, they state that they are committed to protecting the rights and legitimate interests of the citizens of their countries
who have to shoulder the burden caused by the immigration of European citizens who actually fail to meet the requirements. Thirdly, they
express their commitment to preventing and combating the fraudulent
use of the right of free movement of Union citizens or by third country
nationals abusing free movement rights in order to circumvent national
immigration controls. This language, designed in 2013, finds its way into
the draft Decision of the Heads of State and Government of 19 February
2016 to satisfy the demands of the British Prime Minister to campaign
for a vote (in a referendum he has called) for the UK to remain in the EU.

In this April 2013 letter, four types of people are identified: (1) 'real'
citizens – nationals of the Member States and who are not required to
fulfil any conditions at home but in whose name the interior ministers
are acting, (2) Union citizens who enjoy that title because they comply

with EU secondary legislation as understood by the interior ministers, (3) European citizens who are really immigrants because they fail to meet the requirements and (4) Union citizens and their third country nationals (family members) who are fraudulently using and abusing EU free movement rights to avoid national laws. The wrong type of people – categories three and four – according to the ministers threaten the ministers' common goal of strengthening cohesion in the host communities by integrating new immigrants. This common goal, once again transforms even 'good' Union citizens into new immigrants, rather than real citizens. If they were 'real' citizens then they would be entitled not to integrate if they chose. But if they are really immigrants, then it is reasonable to expect them to integrate (whatever might be meant by that term).

Further, according to the interior ministers, the wrong kind of immigrants place an excessive strain on the social systems of the receiving states thereby threatening the acceptance of the European idea of solidarity. The ministers call for more powers to act against these bad immigrants, including re-entry bans applicable from expulsion, clearer rules on the measures which can be taken to counter fraud and abuse, marriages of convenience. Additionally, the interior ministers demand powers to exclude from entitlement to social benefits those who have not been employed or paid taxes in the host State. Finally, the four interior ministers criticise other Member States (presumably but not specified, the EU 8, Bulgaria and Romania) for their treatment of their own citizens and demand that they take steps to permanently improve living conditions of their own citizens. The four interior ministers go so far as to imply that some of these states are themselves acting fraudulently: "we call on them [those other Member States who remain nameless but who know who they are] to make sure that the EU funds which have already been set aside for these purposes are actually used to benefit those concerned."

One of the striking features of the demands is that although they are made by interior ministers, and most of the demands are actually in fields of activity of the social affairs and labour ministries which are not associated with the letter. Further, the interior ministers are clear that they are acting in the interests, primarily if not exclusively, of their own citizens, nationals of their state, not EU citizens in general. Their entitlement to act to protect their own nationals in fields outside the responsibility of their ministries is based on their appreciation of the need for integration of Union citizens into their communities. As Union citizens, nationals of other Member States are actually perceived by these ministers as immigrants the logic is that their rights should be defined by the host Mem-

ber State in the interests of the protection of their own nationals with
the objective that these Union citizens should become as like their own
nationals (or at least the right kind of their own nationals) as quickly as
possible (integration). The entitlement to remain an EU citizen enjoying
EU rights in a host Member State is outside this form of logic. The ministers' unspoken demon is diversity – the EU principle that diversity is a
strength[6] is rejected entirely when it comes to people.

The VISEGRAD group of EU Member States from Central and Eastern
Europe expressed their full support for the rights of EU citizens at the
following Council meeting and the Commission requested information
from the four Member States regarding the exact nature and scale of the
problems which they identified in their letter.

Managing Monstrous Fears: Expertise

The fears expressed by the interior ministers in their letter to the Presidency in April 2013 and which have formed the basis of a number of the
UK demands in the negotiations leading to the draft Decision of 19 February 2016 needed to be addressed. The institution best placed to deal
with the response is of course the Commission which did so in a Com-
munication of November 2013.[7] The mechanism which the Commission
used was expertise. It requested detailed information from the Member
States and EUROSTAT, the EU statistical agency, regarding the claims and
concerns expressed in the April 2013 letter. On the basis of the information which it received, the Commission produced a very full but read-
able rebuttal to the claims of the four interior ministers. The Commission
noted that free movement of EU workers has existed since the 1960s. It
reminded the Member States that it had provided them with guidance
on the citizens directive in 2009 and had already resolved 90% of trans-
position issues with Member States regarding the directive. It pointed to
evidence of the positive effects on economies of free movement of workers and reminded everyone that this is one of the four fundamental freedoms of the internal market. It presented its research indicating that free
movement of workers in the period 2004 – 2009 (following the accession

---

6   Article 167(1) TFEU "1. The Union shall contribute to the flowering of the cultures
        of the Member States, while respecting their national and regional diversity and at
        the same time bringing the common cultural heritage to the fore."

7   COM(2013)837 final.

the kind of information provided to it by the United Kingdom shows the type of exceptional situation that the proposed safeguard mechanism is intended to cover exists in the United Kingdom today. Accordingly, the United Kingdom would be justified in triggering the mechanism in the full expectation of obtaining approval." This mechanism would not only reverse the rights of EU citizens by limiting their entitlement to move and reside in the UK but it would constitute the abandonment of one of the four freedoms on which the internal market is built, but for one Member State in particular. Further, as discussed in section 2 above, the Commission appeared to fetter its own discretion regarding the assessment of the possible need to trigger such a mechanism at the time when the request might be made by already indicating that it was satisfied that the conditions were fulfilled. The authority of the Commission was deeply compromised by this draft declaration.

In the final version of the draft declaration of the Commission attached to the draft Decision of 19 February 2016, one amendment was made. The Commission states that in its decision that the UK was entitled to trigger the mechanism (at some time in the future) it took into account the fact that "in particular as [the UK] has not made full use of the transitional periods on free movement of workers which were provided for in the recent Accession Acts..." The suggestion which is apparent from this wording is that the mechanism might be triggered in a variable manner – against citizens of the EU 8, Bulgaria and Romania but not against the pre-2004 Member States. If this was the intention then the Commission was complicit also in institutionalising inequality among Union citizens. Further, the additional wording seems to indicate that if a Member State did not use transitional restrictions on free movement of workers to the full during the original period after accession of a new Member State, then this would be a ground for that Member State to use restrictions afterwards. It is as if transitional restrictions could be put, like money, into the bank and withdrawn in bits later when the politicians of the day were spooked by anti-free movement campaigners.

In the transformation of EU citizens into dangerous immigrants, the British Prime Minister demanded more powers to expel EU citizens from the UK. This had also been a demand of the four interior ministers in April 2013, concerned as they were at the time about the arrival of the wrong kind of EU immigrants who place strains on their communities. Expulsion is perhaps the most dramatic of actions a state can take to indicate to a person that they are not a citizen and are unwanted in the host State. Thus the rules on the expulsion of EU citizens from a host Member

State were tightened up in 2004 in the citizens directive giving ever greater protection to EU citizens against this violence after five and again after
ten years of residence in the host State. Indeed after ten years residence
an EU citizen can only be expelled on imperative grounds of public security. Further according to the citizens directive previous criminal con-
victions shall not in themselves constitute grounds for taking expulsion
measures. Only the personal conduct of the individual concerned can be
taken into account when a host State is considering expulsion and the
person must represent a genuine, present and sufficiently serious threat
affecting one of the fundamental interests of society.

   This protection in the citizens directive is the result of thirty years of
jurisprudence of the CJEU protecting EU citizens from expulsion on the
basis of unfounded fears or prejudices of public authorities. Yet, when
faced with the demands of the British Prime Minister the Commission
included in its draft declaration on issues related to the abuse of the right
of free movement of persons attached to the President of the Council's
letter of 2 February and unchanged in the Council Conclusions of 19 February 2016, new promises to allow Member States to expel EU citizens.
Specifically the Commission promised that it would clarify (which appears to mean no actual change of the citizens directive only the issue of
some clarification) that Member States may take into account past conduct of an individual in the determination of whether the citizen poses
a "present" threat to public policy or security. It also undertook to permit
host Member States to expel EU citizens on preventative grounds even
in the absence of a previous criminal conviction. In the event of a future
revision of the citizens directive, the Commission agreed to include the
new thresholds for expulsion. This is a promise to put EU law into reverse
and to take away from citizens rights which they had already acquired,
normally a prohibited zone for EU law as an affront to the ever closer union which is the objective of the EU. The distance between equality of EU
citizens and discrimination on the basis of nationality also widened with
this undertaking of the Commission. No longer would EU citizens be entitled to the same treatment as regards suspicion and prejudice regarding
their activities. The criminal justice system of a Member State would no
longer be the arbiter of whether a crime had been committed and an EU
citizen culprit should be punished.[11] Instead, the administrative authorities, on the basis of their suspicions could seek to expel an EU citizen.

---

11   Mitsilegas, Valsamis. *EU Criminal Law After Lisbon: Rights, Trust and the Transfor-
      mation of Justice in Europe.* Bloomsbury Publishing, 2016.

The criminal justice standard and burden of proof (beyond reasonable doubt) would no longer hinder expulsion of an EU citizen as expulsion would be an administrative matter taken in the absence of a criminal conviction on the balance of probabilities standard of administrative law.

The fears of administrators regarding an EU citizen would be justified as a ground for his or her expulsion from the host State. This would then reinforce the sense of conviction (and impunity) of administrators to act in the best interests of their (real) citizens by expelling EU citizens who seem dodgy. The Commission once again betrayed EU citizens in the interests of mollifying a terrified Member State which was wallowing in its monstrous fears.

Conclusions

In an infamous speech by one of the leaders of the Leave campaign, the UK's former Justice Minister, Michael Gove, he stated that "the British people had had enough of experts".[12] The mainstream media was aghast by the treatment of expertise by the Leave campaign leaders.[13] Yet, the British public appeared to be delighted at this new permission by a member of the Cabinet to disregard knowledge, statistics and informed opinion. Instead, ignorance and prejudice were offered as alternatives by the Leave campaigners. This ignorance and prejudice was justified on the basis of fears and anxieties which were protected from contradiction by any form of knowledge or expertise, irrespective of the exemplary qualifications of its source. Because a Leave voter was fearful and encouraged to be fearful by those with the titles of respectable political leaders, he or she was entitled to disregard all truth claims and all knowledge produced by reputable sources of expertise.

The EU institutions and the other Member States were complicit in this inversion of expertise. While they had insisted on evidence-led policy making in the field of free movement of workers only two years earlier, now in the face of threats by the British Prime Minister that he would campaign in favour of leaving the EU, they accepted a series of proposals which flew in the face of all evidence about free movement of workers. One discards evidence-led policy making at one's peril. When public

---

12   https://www.youtube.com/watch?v=GGgiGtJk7MA visited 30 August 2016.

13   https://www.ft.com/content/3be49734-29cb-11e6-83e4-abc22d5d1o8c visited 30
      August 2016.

policy is no longer discussed, argued and judged on the basis of evidence it is rapidly debased. There is no longer a threshold against which claims can be tested in accordance with commonly accepted standards regarding the creation of truth and its reflection of external reality. Instead, public policy becomes hostage to monstrous fears and the principal tools capable of reigning in those fears, knowledge and truth, have been discredited.

Conclusions

A myth is a kind of story told in public,
which people tell one another;
they wear an air of ancient wisdom,
but that is part of their seductive charm.

MARINA WARNER, *Managing Monsters: Six Myths of Our Time – The Reith*
Lectures, 1994

In this book, I have examined the results of the UK's BREXIT referendum from the perspective of citizenship and the rights of citizens. There is much that remains to be said and undoubtedly colleagues are working on books which will illuminate many other aspects of the developments which have lead to the result that the UK will leave the EU.[1] I have taken the metaphor of the monster as a way to understand what has happened and how the various actors, many of whom should have known better, became complicit in this bonfire of rights. I explained my monsters in the introduction and I will permit myself the luxury of repetition only in one regard – that of St George and his dragon. St George, the symbol of England, is depicted vanquishing his monstrous dragon. In English religious (and political) imagery, St George is the hero freeing his people (the English) from a monstrous tyrant. This motif was played and replayed by the Leave camp in the referendum campaign. But if one changes the theological framework of St George and his dragon to that of the 19th century Haitians, the dragon is the god to be venerated who is going through the act of sacrifice necessary for his deification after the creation of the world. St George is of no interest except as a poor tool. The Haitian take on St George and the dragon was not much in evidence in the BREXIT campaign. Yet if one leaves theology altogether and we return to the stories we tell our children so that they will understand the world, toads may be princes once kissed, beasts may be the beloved objects of beauties, Europa loved her monstrous bull and gave her name to our continent.

In the second section I reviewed the negotiations between the EU institutions and the UK which led to the new settlement for the UK in the EU which the EU Member States and institutions offered the UK Prime Minister to convince him to campaign to remain in the EU. There is

---

1   There are of course still experts who think that this outcome may be avoided. It is
     not for me to pass judgment on the matter.

something astonishingly grotesque about these negotiations. In the first
instance, it was the same Prime Minister who had decided, in the short
term interests of his faction of his political party to call a referendum on
whether to remain or leave the EU. He had announced this at least as
early as 2013. But once he had put in place his legislation for the referendum, he then menaced the EU institutions and the other Member States
that if they did not play by his ridiculously short time frame and give him
everything which his advisers were able to think up (almost chosen as
punishments for past EU institutional insubordination to UK positions
on citizens' un-rights) he would campaign to leave the EU. Secondly, the
capitulations which the British Prime Minister extracted from the EU
institutions and Member States (one cannot speak of compromises as
there was no compromise at all on the UK side) were monstrous betray-
als of the most base kind of EU citizens, the EU treaties, the CJEU and
rule of law. Thirdly, the arrogance of the British Government in the negotiations was monstrous – the sense of entitlement to treat the other 27
Member States and the institutions as inferior is palpable in each letter
and demand from the British Prime Minister. Finally, the willingness of
the other Member States and EU institutions to participate in this cha-
rade has brought disgrace on them.

In the third section I investigated the question of monstrous citizenships. The British dismissal of EU citizenship and what appears to be a
policy of the British negotiators to undermine as far as possible even the
concept of EU citizenship by emptying it of rights, is only a mirror image
of what the UK Government had already done to British citizenship. The
transformation of citizenship into a paltry type of immigration status
had already taken place in the UK. Why not apply the same approach to
EU citizenship? The idea that EU citizens should have rights, and even indeed fundamental rights set out in a Charter was clearly insulting to the
British side. More than once, they complained explicitly about this fact.
With an impressive lack of courage, the British Supreme Court turned
its back on EU citizenship and the rights which it promised, even where
limited to the entitlement to a proportionality assessment before the
withdrawal of British citizenship. British sovereignty, to be repatriated
to the UK through the departure from the EU, means that citizens have
no rights except the right to be obedient to the power of the day, or be
deprived of citizenship altogether.

In the fourth section I unravel the fear of our public administrations
regarding the contamination of the people by reason of marriage to the
wrong kind – the foreigners (all of whom are would-be immigrants in this

logic). The extraordinary lengths to which state authorities are willing to go, in particular the British ones, to make family life difficult, expensive and unattainable for these disobedient citizens who marry third country nationals, almost defies belief. This fear and horror is dragged into the centre of the BREXIT debate as the British Prime Minister demands that the whole of the EU must share his horror of these contaminating couples and transform EU law on family reunion to reflect the British rules. It would seem that some Member States were already willing to abandon themselves (and any good sense which they may have had left) in the British fears about the wrong types of families but these were not so many. Instead the British negotiators demands ever more compromising undertakings from the EU institutions to enable UK authorities to refuse residence to the third country national family members of their own citizens who might seek to move back to the UK.

In the fifth and final substantive section, I reflect on the monstrous fears which drove the BREXIT campaign and how the other Member States and the EU institutions ended up pandering to those fears. The role of expertise, knowledge and their claims to reveal truth were trammelled under foot. Even the most respected of authorities such as the International Monetary Fund and most highly regarded of institutions such as the British Office for National Statistics were reviled and ridiculed as inaccurate and/or irrelevant. The term 'post-truth' has been coined to describe this political use of lies as better than evidence and truth.[2] Instead of evidence, apparently respectable politicians encouraged the British public to revel in monstrous fears and to stop their ears against the experts. Politics itself was debased and degraded by this midsummer night's madness. As in Shakespeare's play, ordinary folk suddenly seemed to have been captured in magic spells where their heads were transformed into those of donkeys and they dreamed they were adored by fairy queens.

The referendum is over and the result, though not overwhelming, has been accepted by all the institutions as binding. One might consider this somewhat odd when both the Irish (twice) and the Danes (once) have been invited to think and vote again. When the people of these two countries did reconsider their negative EU votes, they changed their minds. No such option is available for the British. Neither the British Government nor any of the EU institutions or other Member State have even entertained the possibility. The mantra is that the British people have spoken

---

2   Keyes, Ralph. *The post-truth era: Dishonesty and deception in contemporary life.* Macmillan, 2004.

and their choice will be respected. At the time of writing at the end of September 2016, it seems likely that the departure procedure foreseen by Article 50 TEU will commence in early 2017.[3] The constitutional debate in the UK parliament regarding what entity is entitled to trigger the exit procedure is likely to be short-circuited by the Government taking the move and that move being accepted by the EU institutions. This will be yet another example of the solemnity of the (former) Prime Minister's concerns expressed in the negotiations for greater control by national parliaments of EU business.

In the aftermath of the referendum, the British pound dropped in value significantly against the euro and has not recovered. The Bank of England, according to its Governor who gave evidence to parliament in September, has taken exceptional measures to ensure liquidity and to avoid a market slump (including a pronounced new programme of asset purchase by the Bank). The longer term consequences of these measures are likely to be a rise in inflation. In the Council meeting in Bratislava on 16 September 2016, the UK was not invited. At the meeting, the Presidency and the EU institutional actors pointedly referred to the EU of 27 Member States (the 28th, the UK, was already being effaced). The UK's presidency of the EU which was planned for the second half of 2017 has been suspended.[4] For the moment, there is no public information on what the position of the British Government will be on any issue of departure from the EU.

The British media is, in general, triumphalist about the referendum outcome.[5] One is reminded of the thesis of Conor Gearty's book, *Fantasy Island*[6] on the UK and human rights – the resolute refusal to acknowledge the obvious seems to be a particularly enduring characteristic of much if not all of the UK media (the Scots tend to call this 'thinking pink' a reference to the mindset expressed by pre-1960 world maps where large parts of the world were coloured pink evidencing their status as British colonies). When the Governor of the Bank of England gave evi-

---

3   There is currently pending a legal challenge regarding the UK constitutional re-
     quirements for the triggering of the provision http://www.independent.co.uk/
     news/uk/politics/brexit-peoples-challenge-legal-high-court-block-article-50-refer-
     endum-a7335201.html visited 29 September 2016.

4   UK renounces EU presidency http://www.ft.com/cms/s/0/9dfa35aa-4e5b-11e6-
     8172-e39ecd3b86fc.html#axzz4LSrgU8Rz.

5   http://www.express.co.uk/news/politics/682969/nigel-farage-independence-day-
     brexit visited 29 September 2016.

6   Gearty, Conor. "On fantasy island: Britain Strasbourg and human rights." (2016).

dence to the House of Commons Treasury Committee on 7 September he was subjected to a variety of insults from Members of Parliament regarding his forecast, before the referendum, that a leave vote would harm the economy. These Members of Parliament insisted that the economic indicators of the UK are even better now than before the vote. The Governor's efforts to explain that between the short-term measures taken by the Bank of England to avoid an immediate slump and the longer term economic prognosis for the country a gap was widening was ridiculed by those same Members of Parliament. The (current) Prime Minister has consistently refused to give any comfort to non-British EU citizens living in the UK or to British citizens living in other Member States that she will seek to protect their residence and work rights. Uncertainty is the order of the day for everyone who is currently a non-British EU citizen living in the UK. British citizens living in other EU Member States have, for the moment at least, been left to their own devices by their government.

The hope that the future of a UK outside the EU will be tied to the USA remains uncertain. At the Bratislava Council meeting of 16 September the new priorities of the EU were set out, one of which is internal and external security. On 8 July 2016 the Presidents of the European Council, the Commission and the Secretary General of NATO signed a joint declaration signalling the need for new ways of working together.[7] The new external security defence priority declared in Bratislava raises questions about the EU's way forward in defence. It is unlikely that this item would have been on the table let alone selected as a priority if the British negotiators had been there. It raises the thorny question of the relationship of NATO and the EU, generally unwelcome to US interests, which are bound up with a one vehicle, NATO approach. The consequences of this possible change of direction in European defence policy may have implications for the UK-US relationship as recognised by the British Defence Secretary Michael Fallon.[8] A UK outside an EU but inside NATO when European defence policy is moving elsewhere may be less interesting to the US.

The integrity of the UK appears to be on hold at the moment (September 2016). The Scottish Nationalist Party's leader, Nicola Sturgeon, has let

---

7   http://www.nato.int/cps/en/natohq/official_texts_133163.htm visited 29 September 2016.

8   http://www.express.co.uk/news/politics/714812/Defence-Secretary-Michael-Fallon-block-EU-army-Germany-France-plans-Bratislava-meeting visited 29 September 2016.

it be known that the UK's departure from the EU may be a reason to trigger a second independence referendum so that Scotland could remain in the EU but no practical steps have been taken. Rather more quietly some discussions have been taking place between actors in Northern Ireland and the Republic about how to manage BREXIT not least regarding border controls and security.

It is still early days following the referendum but one thing is clear – the UK is set to leave the EU. The UK's participation in an EU project based on free movement of goods, persons, services and capital will soon be over. The British political and public gaze is likely to become both more internally and US focussed (though whether the US will reciprocate is unclear). Once again, in the British imagination, the continent is likely to be cut off because of fog in the Channel.[9]

---

9   http://www.thetimes.co.uk/article/fog-in-channel-brexiteers-isolated-from-brit-
      ains-duty-to-save-europe-7pv5k6c9b visited 29 September 2016.

Bibliography

Amos, Merris. *Human Rights Law*. Bloomsbury Publishing, 2014.

Bellamy, Richard, and Alex Warleigh-Lack. "From an Ethics of Integration to an Ethics of Participation: Citizenship and the Future of the European Union." *Millennium: A Journal of International Studies* 27 (1998): 447-70.

Bigo, Didier. "Rethinking Security at the crossroad of International Relations and Criminology." *British Journal of Criminology* (2016): azw062.

Bigo, Didier. "Reflections on Immigration Controls and Free Movement in Europe." *Constructing and Imagining Labour Migration: Perspectives of Control from Five Continents* (2016): 293.

Closa, Carlos. "The concept of citizenship in the treaty on European Union." *Common Market Law Review* 29.6 (1992): 1137-1169.

Costello, Cathryn. "Metock: free movement and "normal family life" in the Union." *Common Market law review* 46.2 (2009): 587-622.

Douglas-Scott, Sionaidh. "A UK Exit from the EU: The End of the United Kingdom or a New Constitutional Dawn?." *Cambridge Journal of International and Comparative Law* (2015).

Dummett, Ann. *The Acquisition of British Citizenship. From Imperial Traditions to National Definitions*. na, 1994.

Gearty, Conor. *On fantasy island: Britain Strasbourg and human rights* (2016).

Goodwin-Gill, Guy S. International Law and the Movement of Persons between States (1978), 212-26.

Gower, Melanie. "Deprivation of British citizenship and withdrawal of passport facilities." *House of Commons Library, SN/HA/6820 (www. parliament. uk/business/publications/research/briefing-papers/SN06820/deprivation-ofbritish-citizenship-and-withdrawal-of-passportfacilities)* (2014).

Groenendijk, Kees. "Family reunification as a right under community law." *European Journal of Migration and Law* 8.2 (2006): 215.

Guild, Elspeth. "Free Movement of EU Citizens and their Family Members" New Journal of European Criminal Law 2(2016): 34.

Harlow, Carol. "Editorial: Transparency, Accountability and the Privileges of Power." *European Law Journal* 22.3 (2016): 273-278.

Infantino, Federica. "Bordering 'fake' marriages? The everyday practices of control at the consulates of Belgium, France and Italy in Casablanca." *Etnografia e ricerca qualitativa* 7.1 (2014): 27-48.

Keyes, Ralph. *The post-truth era: Dishonesty and deception in contemporary life*. Macmillan, 2004.

Lenaerts, Koen. "Exploring the limits of the EU Charter of Fundamental Rights." *European Constitutional Law Review* 8.03 (2012): 375-403.

Lowe, Vaughan. "The Iraq Crisis: What Now?." *International and Comparative Law Quarterly* 52.04 (2003): 859-871.

MacDonald, Ian Alexander, and Ronan Toal, eds. *Macdonald's Immigration law and practice*. 2015.

MacShane Denis *BREXIT, How Britain Left Europe* IB Taurus, London 2016.

Mantu, Sandra. *Contingent Citizenship: The Law and Practice of Citizenship Deprivation in International, European and National Perspectives*. Brill, 2015.

Martin, D. "Comments on Forster (Case C-158/07 of 18 November 2008), Metock (Case C-127/08 of 25 July 2008) and Huber (Case C-524/06 of 16 December 2008)." *Eur. J. Migration & L.* 11 (2009): 95.

Métraux, Alfred. *Voodoo in Haiti*. Vol. 341. Schocken, 1972.

Mitsilegas, Valsamis. *EU Criminal Law After Lisbon: Rights, Trust and the Transformation of Justice in Europe*. Bloomsbury Publishing, 2016.

Patel, Hasu H. "General Amin and the Indian exodus from Uganda." *Issue: A Journal of Opinion* 2.4 (1972): 12-22.

Pech, Laurent 'The European Union's Lisbon Treaty: Some Thoughts on the 'Irish Legal Guarantees'" http://www.ejiltalk.org/the-european-unions-lisbon-treaty-some-thoughts-on-the-irish-legal-guarantees/ visited 12 August 2016.

Peers, Steve, et al., eds. *The EU Charter of fundamental rights: a commentary*. Bloomsbury Publishing, 2014.

Poptcheva, E-M and D Eatock *The UK's 'new' settlement' in the European Union* EPRS PE 577.983.

Ryan, Bernard F. "Integration requirements: A new model in migration law." (2008).

Shaw, Jo. "The interpretation of European Union citizenship." *The Modern Law Review* 61.3 (1998): 293-317.

Tandon, Yash. "The expulsions from Uganda: Asians' role in East Africa." *Patterns of Prejudice* 6.6 (1972): 1-8.

Walker, Rob BJ. *Out of Line: Essays on the Politics of Boundaries and the Limits of Modern Politics*. Routledge, 2015.

Warner, Marina. "Six myths of our time: Managing monsters." *The Reith Lectures* 4 (1994).

Wiener, Antje, and Vincent Della Sala. "Constitution-making and Citizenship Practice–Bridging the Democracy Gap in the EU?." *JCMS: Journal of Common Market Studies* 35.4 (1997): 595-614.

Wilson, Wendy. "EU migrants: entitlement to housing assistance (England)." *House of Commons Library Standard Note* (2016).

Wintemute, Robert, and Mads Tønnesson Andenæs, eds. *Legal recognition of same-sex partnerships: A study of national, European and international law.* Hart Publishing, 2001.

Wray, Helena. *Regulating marriage migration into the UK: A stranger in the home.* Ashgate Publishing, Ltd., 2011.